CREATING GREAT DESIGNS ON A LIMITED BUDGET

LEE CHARTIER

&

SCOTT MASON

NORTH LIGHT BOOKS
CINCINNATI, OHIO

Library of Congress Cataloging-in-Publication Data

Chartier, Lee,
    Creating great designs on a limited budget / Lee Chartier & Scott Mason.
        p. cm.
    Includes index.
    ISBN 0-89134-607-4
    1. Graphic arts—United States—Design. I. Mason, Scott. II. Title.

TT853.C49 1995   95-1798
746.6—dc20   CIP

Edited by Lynn Haller
Designed by Angela Lennert

The permissions on page iii constitute an extension of this copyright page.

About the Authors

Lee Chartier is a professor at the Community College of Rhode Island where she teaches marketing-related courses. Previously, she served as Director of Public Relations and Publications at the Community College for eight years, managing the production of promotional and informational materials. She also worked at Rhode Island School of Design and as an art director at a Rhode Island advertising agency. Chartier holds a bachelor's degree from Brown University and a master's degree from the University of Rhode Island.

Scott Mason is partner in a design firm in Providence, Rhode Island. His firm specializes in graphic design for nonprofit human services organizations, arts groups, art institutions, educational institutions and health-related organizations. He has never once heard a client say "Money is no object."

Dedication

This book is dedicated to my grandmother, artist Ella Rex Price, for inspiring me with her love of the visual arts, and to the people I love the most—Jack, Kate and Christopher Chartier, whose support has made this book possible.

—Lee M. Chartier

And to Ant, who has fed me figuratively and literally for over ten years.

—Scott Mason

Acknowledgments

Special thanks to Lynn Haller for her tireless assistance as well as to all of the talented designers who have generously shared their work with us to feature in this book.

Permissions

Contents

MARGAY
(FELIS WEIDII)

HIGH IN THE CANOPY OF THE SOUTH AMERICAN RAIN FOREST, THE MARGAY LEAPS AND CLIMBS THROUGH THE TREES, LIKE A TRAPEZE ARTIST PLAYING TO AN AUDIENCE. THIS LITTLE CREATURE IS ONE OF THE MOST AGILE AMONG THE CATS. ITS FEET ARE MUCH WIDER AND MORE FLEXIBLE THAN THOSE OF ITS RELATIVES, AND IT HAS THE ABILITY TO ROTATE ITS HIND FEET A FULL 180 DEGREES. WITH LONG STEELY CLAWS, THE MARGAY IS A FORMIDABLE ADVERSARY. WHEN IT COMES OUT AT NIGHT TO HUNT, IT HAS ITS CHOICE OF MANY SMALL ANIMALS.

NEEDLESS TO SAY, SCIENTISTS HAVE A HARD TIME KEEPING UP WITH THE MARGAY TO STUDY IT IN THE WILD. AS A RESULT, LITTLE IS KNOWN ABOUT THE CAT'S HABITS. WHAT WE DO KNOW, HOWEVER, IS THAT SOME HUMANS HAVE MANAGED TO CATCH UP WITH THE ELUSIVE CREATURE. THE MARGAY'S SLEEK COAT CAN BE FOUND IN FURS ALL OVER THE WORLD. RECENTLY, TOUGHER INTERNATIONAL CONTROLS HAVE RESTRICTED THE FUR TRADE, PROTECT- ING THE BEAUTIFUL YELLOW AND BLACK COAT OF THE MARGAY. YET, IT MAY NOT BE ENOUGH. LOSS OF HABITAT CONTINUES TO THREATEN THE LITTLE CAT, LEAVING THE ACROBAT NO PLACE TO CLIMB AND LEAP.

The zookeepers call her Little Girl. This beautiful margay was still considered a kitten when she was rescued by the Fish and Wildlife Department. She was being smuggled in the trunk of a car over the Mexican border in Brownsville, Texas. Now, she's almost old enough to have kittens of her own.

When Pat Callahan was growing up he had unusual domestic animals as pets. Now he has an exotic cat in his care that can be friendly and playful one moment, aloof and mischievous the next. He says it keeps him on his toes.

Chapter Two: The Power of Limited-Color Design

In this chapter, you'll find out what simple graphic elements will help you make the most of your one- or two-color designs.

Chapter Three: Inexpensive Visuals

In this chapter, you'll find out how you can get the visuals you need to make your piece work, without paying an illustrator.

Chapter Four: Low-Cost Production and Printing

This chapter will teach you how to get your piece produced, printed, and bound as inexpensively as possible.

Chapter Five: More Great Designs on a Limited Budget

In this chapter, you'll see more examples of designers who made the most of limited resources.

Index

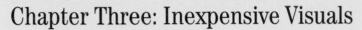

Introduction

Designing a communications piece that effectively conveys an appropriate message to a specific audience is a challenging task, one that's certainly made easier by costly special effects and full-color images. But as we move away from an era of excessive spending towards a time of belt-tightening and efficiency, designers who can produce a beautiful and effective piece within the confines of a limited budget are in greater demand than ever before. Learning how to create great designs on a limited budget is more crucial than ever—thus the need for this book.

Because the phrase "limited budget" means different things to different people, this book includes the work of designers who have solved communications problems in an efficient manner. Though all were considered "limited budget" by their designers, some of these pieces might be beyond your own budget. Nevertheless, the principles they employ may point you in a direction that will help you solve your own design problems.

Chapter one reviews the basic elements of great limited budget design. You'll find out how to tap your creative powers to come up with a concept that will communicate your message to your audience. Then you'll discover how to use visuals, simplicity, contrast and surprise to translate these ideas into a great design.

Since a limited budget usually means a restricted use of color, chapter two focuses on the elements of effective one- and two-color design. You'll learn how to use type and photography for maximum impact. Abstract graphics and line art can also create dramatic effects, and you'll find out how to use them in new ways to support your message.

In chapter three you'll discover exciting new ways to create your own visuals, how to find and use photos inexpensively, and how to find copyright-free visuals.

Once you've developed your concept and designed your piece, you'll want to know how to produce it without breaking the bank. Chapter four provides you with cost-cutting strategies that will help you save money on production, color, paper, printing and binding.

Finally, chapter five gives you more examples of great work done on a limited budget, to give you inspiration as you work on your own limited-budget projects.

The ideas compiled here will both stimulate your imagination and give you practical information about how to turn your own ideas into great designs inexpensively. But this book doesn't attempt to be the last word on this subject; take this as a starting point, but continue to learn as much as you can about design, illustration, photography and production and printing techniques. Knowledge is the best tool to save money on all your design projects.

Chapter One
The Elements of Great Designs on a Limited Budget

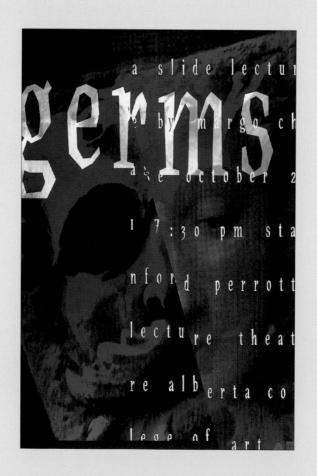

With access to an unlimited budget, almost any designer can create an adequate piece. It's easy enough to hide a lack of talent or a good idea behind the work of a high-priced photographer, or a slick and impressive six-color print job. But it takes real talent to create an unforgettable piece out of nothing more than a good idea, a few well-chosen typefaces and graphics, and a one- or two-color print job. This situation sets the great designers apart from the mediocre ones. Unfortunately, it's also a situation almost all beginning designers, and many experienced designers, must face in a majority of pieces they design.

Rather than viewing a limited budget as a hindrance, think of it as a challenge to get to what's essential about the message of your piece. It's also a great test of the strength of the concept of the piece itself: Is your idea good enough to stand alone and unadorned? A limited budget is the quickest way to expose any inadequacy in this area.

> Learn the basics to great design, whatever your budget.

Designing limited budget pieces is an excellent way to learn to focus on communication, not decoration. Take the lessons you learn from this chapter, and from your limited budget projects, and apply what you learn to projects with larger budgets; your work will be the better for it.

Start with a Strong Idea

A strong idea is the basis for all good design and effective communication. It attracts attention and draws the reader in. A strong idea can stimulate interest, create desire and even motivate action. It makes your message noteworthy and memorable. A strong idea sets you apart from your competitors and allows you to effectively communicate your message to your target audience.

A strong idea is critical to the success of a low budget design project. High-priced work that employs sophisticated production techniques can dazzle readers with a multitude of special effects and colors—possibly distracting them from the lack of a good idea—but you don't have that option when you're designing with limited funds. Fortunately, a good concept is the cheapest design element of all, and the most effective.

The first step in developing a strong idea is determining the intended message of your piece. What is the client trying to communicate to the audience? What is he trying to accomplish? It's a good idea to discuss this with him and, if possible, with others in the organization. They may provide insight and direction that the client, grown too close to the project, is unable to provide himself.

Do, also, keep in mind that "message" doesn't just mean the verbal content of your piece—its look will communicate a secondary message about the organization the piece represents, and should be developed to reinforce your primary message. For instance, a slick, ostentatious publication, if sent by a nonprofit organization to solicit donations, would send a secondary message that would undercut the primary one.

The theme "big experience, small theatre" is carried out visually in the juxtaposition of large and small type and graphics in this brochure for a small theatre company. The brochure used existing theatre publicity photos as visuals, and the piece was economically printed in black and white.

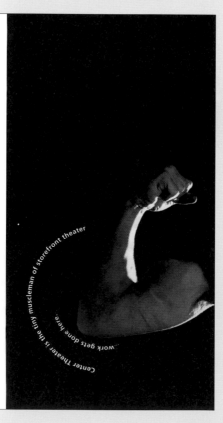

Creating Great Designs on a Limited Budget

This pictogram plays on the client's name by combining simple graphic images of a cat and a man. The simplicity of the execution—a one-color print job with a screen tint—ensures that nothing distracts the viewer from the cleverness of the concept.

Once you know what your message is, you need to know your audience, to understand how your message might best be communicated to them: Is the audience primarily male or female, young or old, educated or uneducated? To find out how they think and what's important to them, you'll need to use simple, inexpensive strategies to collect this information. Your client may be able to provide you with an existing profile or information from past sales records. You could also talk with individuals in the organization who have direct contact with clients. Or, if time allows and if your client permits it, hold an informal focus group with customers so you can meet the audience and ask their opinions about the product or service. Most people will be flattered that you asked for their input; your client might offer group members some small benefit for attending to provide incentive to participate. In any case, a focus group could provide a perspective you might not get otherwise.

Another necessary part of your design background is familiarity with the product or service your piece promotes. Hold it, use it, try it, shop for it, visit it, participate in it—learn as much as you can about it.

Take a look at your competitors to make sure your idea and your piece are distinctive. As always, input from your client is crucial—he or she knows more about the competitors and the market than you could ever hope to learn in a short period of time.

Once you know your client's objectives, audience, product or service, and market, you have the necessary foundation to start brainstorming. This isn't the time to think about

Start with a Strong Idea

financial constraints—imposing restrictions at this point will only eliminate potentially wonderful ideas. Come up with your concept by exploring without limitations; start with the sky as the limit. Then brainstorm—there are never too many ideas to choose from. Don't be afraid to move in unlikely directions; you may find a solution where you weren't looking for one.

In *A Kick in the Seat of the Pants*, Roger vonOech offers some great strategies for unlocking your creative powers. For instance, he suggests putting things in a different context. Imagine unusual "what if" questions. If you're creating a poster for a college theater production, ask yourself: *What if a celebrity came? What if no one came? What if we were reviewed by New York's finest critic?* This may stimulate some interesting ideas. Look for comparisons between your product and other things. Break rules. Poke fun.

Once you've arrived at some possible solutions, challenge yourself further by figuring out how you can execute your idea within the confines of your budget. This may involve some compromise or paring down, but that will only challenge your creativity further. Remember, a fresh and unique outlook will contribute more to the success of your piece than all the elaborate techniques money can buy. There is no substitute for a strong idea.

Things to keep in mind when trying to develop a strong idea:

• Ask yourself these questions: Why is this piece being created? What action do you want the recipient to take? What is most likely to move the recipient to respond?

Stencils and spray paint give this large, inexpensively produced newsprint poster the feel of an urban construction site—an appropriate mood for an invitation to the opening of a studio in an urban location.

Channeling Children's Anger

Child-like crayon scribbling makes a graphic representation of a child's anger being channeled into a positive image. The artwork was created with a black crayon, then printed in red.

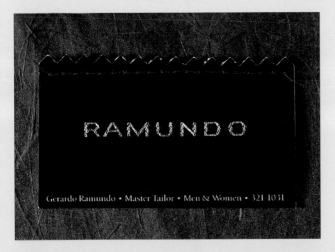

Including actual sewing machine stitching in red is the idea that makes this simple black-and-white business card for a tailor special. Embossing the tailor's name follows through nicely on this concept.

• Find out as much as you can about your audience, including their age, socioeconomic status, where they live, likes and dislikes—all of the factors that will help you develop an idea that speaks to this audience.

• Write down all the words you can think of that pertain to what you're promoting. Put together unlikely combinations of these words to see if they spark an image, phrase or abstract idea. Build on that.

• Randomly pick a word from the dictionary. Try to make a connection between that word and your subject matter; this may conjure up a unique image or may be totally nonsensical. In any case, it will force you to see your subject matter from a different viewpoint.

• Research how others have dealt with similar subject matter. Then take a totally different approach.

• It's not always necessary to visually or verbally depict the thing you're promoting. Think of the sights, sounds, smells, activity or movement that are associated with it, and try to represent them in an abstract or unconventional way.

• Make sure that your idea is appropriate for the subject matter. Avoid using any element that has nothing to do with what you're trying to convey.

• Remember, technique is no substitute for a great idea; your idea should be almost fully developed before you begin thinking about how to execute it.

Start with a Strong Idea

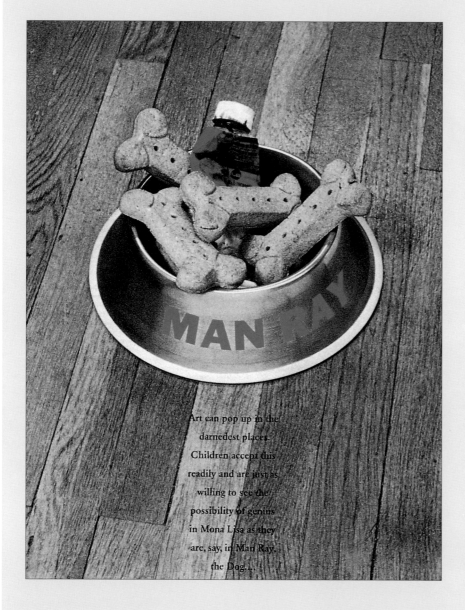

Art can pop up in the darnedest places. Children accept this readily and are just as willing to see the possibility of genius in Mona Lisa as they are, say, in Man Ray, the Dog...

A strong black-and-white photograph creates a visual relationship between a traditional art form—painting—and contemporary photographer William Wegman's dog. To save money, the photograph was taken by the designers.

The company
that has moved
mortgage risk analysis
to a new level
is now moving to
larger quarters.

Using plastic "Monopoly" pieces, the designer created a visual representation
of the company moving into larger quarters. The photograph was taken by the
designer to save the cost of a photographer. The image was manipulated in
Adobe Photoshop and went straight to film.

Start with a Strong Idea

an introduction to
The Heights Schools

diver-
sity
opportunity

quality

involve
ment

innovation

To visually underscore the message that this institution is "people-oriented," the designer uses warm duotones and key words set in large, bright hued type. The kinetics of the design, which incorporates large and small type and graphics, color contrast, and a variety of type treatments and layouts, gives the feeling that there is much activity at this institution. Reversed, ghosted images of the facility are used as a background on each spread, unifying the photos, text and quotes.

"Our public schools have **great resources** for a child like ours who has a **special need.** He was able to be **mainstreamed** in a regular kindergarten with **a superb teacher.** He loves school." DEBORAH VAN KLEEF *One son attends Fairfax Elementary School; Writer*

"The schools help **knit us together** as a community. Building the **playground** at Fairfax has given people a chance to **be closer** and created a **gathering place** for the greater community." DAVID BELL *Three children attend Fairfax Elementary and Roxboro Middle School; Attorney, BP America*

"Taylor Academy has **heightened** our son's **interest in studying** and **self-confidence.** The extra measure of **concern** literally changes young lives for the better." REV. DENNIS NORRIS *Two children attend Coventry Elementary and Taylor Academy; Executive Minister, The Cleveland Baptist Association*

These values shape the education program in the Heights Schools:
•Each child is unique.
•All children can achieve at high levels.
•Children learn in different ways and at different rates.
•An effective program is developmentally appropriate and sensitive to the whole child.
  The result is a rich set of educational opportunities and services to help all children succeed. No two classrooms or schools are identical. Teachers use a variety of techniques from cooperative learning to computers. Teacher teams at the middle schools design their classes for the rapidly changing early adolescent. High-school students may choose from more than 200 courses and 80 extracurricular activities. A variety of special services help the schools serve individual needs.

opportunity

involvement

Healthy public institutions have involved citizens. Heights residents value education and support their schools with their time, care, expertise, and money.
  Residents volunteer in the classroom and levy campaigns. They organize ad hoc groups to address specific concerns. Booster clubs support student activities such as music and sports.
  The schools encourage parents to be partners in the education process. Citizens have opportunities to affect education policy at the school and district levels.
  Each school has a PTA that mobilizes parents. Community organizations such as Reaching Heights and individual school foundations cultivate private resources for the public schools.

"There are so **many people** who are **active** and **committed.** Schools are **special** when people are really **involved.**" SHIRLEY GREER *One daughter attends Monticello Middle School*

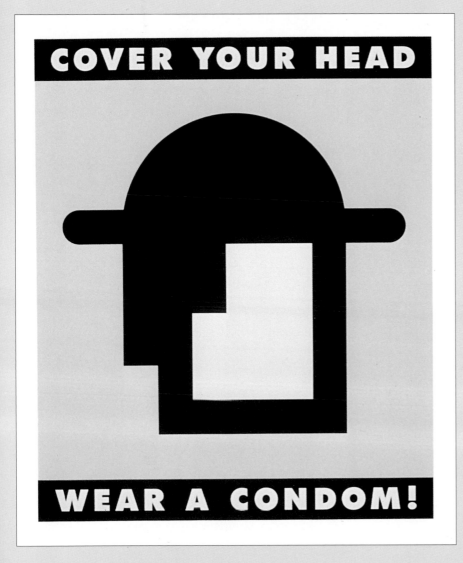

COVER YOUR HEAD

WEAR A CONDOM!

A clever, attention-getting double entendre is used to convey an important message. The simple graphics and the combination of black and high visibility yellow lend this piece the immediacy of a traffic sign.

Powerful Visuals

A powerful visual image serves a twofold purpose in an effective printed piece. First, a great visual initially attracts the intended audience to the piece, catching the eye and generating interest. You often have only seconds in which to captivate and engage your reader; strong images accomplish this quicker than lengthy verbal messages.

Second, a strong visual makes an emotional impact on the reader and creates a recognizable identity for the message and its sponsor, setting the tone for the rest of the piece.

In selecting visuals for your design, keep in mind that they may be used to either explain or reinforce verbal messages, or they can create interest through contrast.

Visuals that complement written messages clarify or expand upon the words. Studies indicate that while some of us prefer to receive messages verbally, others seem to understand things better when they are communicated visually: for instance, some people prefer a map to written directions. Using visuals will help you deliver your message more effectively to this audience. And when used in combination with a verbal message, the graphic will serve as a focal point, attracting the reader's attention and reinforcing the verbal message. The combination of words and images, when used successfully, is greater than the sum of the individual parts—helping you to communicate more effectively with all audiences.

Visuals can also create interest through their apparent contrast with the written message. They can be used to make mundane words majestic or to make grandiose words more grounded. For example, when you

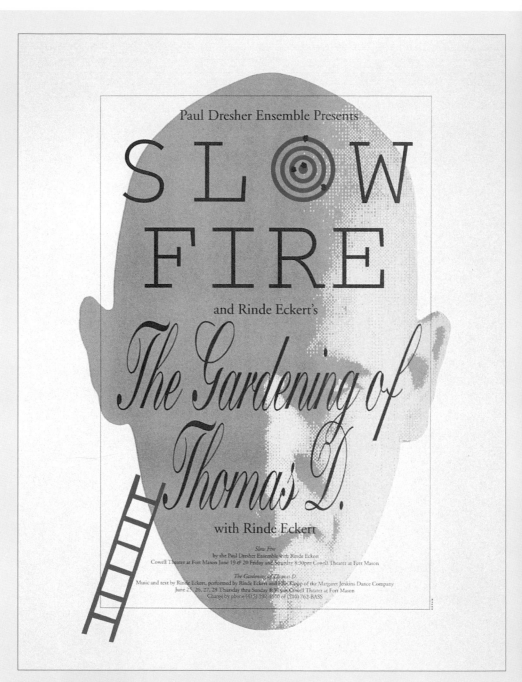

A head is given enormous scale by contrasting a small graphic of a step ladder, almost as if one would have to climb the ladder in order to address the person. This poster was printed in three colors, with the face a ghosted black halftone printed over solid yellow.

Creating Great Designs on a Limited Budget

THE LEGAL AID SOCIETY
OF SAN FRANCISCO
75TH ANNIVERSARY

A large photograph of a pair of chain cutters and a severed chain is a powerful black-and-white image that makes the concept of freedom concrete and immediate. The newspaper clippings that border the photo lend weight and history to the booklet.

greatly enlarge common objects that are part of your message, they take on a grand look. Or, if your message or service is very complex or lofty, a strong visual can simplify it and enhance its appeal to a broader audience.

Visuals can also be used to help organize complicated or lengthy copy. If you're using a single, dominant visual element in your piece, consider using a similar image in a reduced size to highlight important points within the written message. This will break up the copy and help the reader move through it more efficiently.

The use of a powerful visual element need not add considerably to the cost of your design, but it can add significantly to its effectiveness.

Some ways to use visuals effectively:

• Layer type over an image that reinforces its message.

• Use illustration to interpret an abstract idea that would be difficult to convey in words or photographs.

• Use small line-art visuals or dingbats to emphasize and separate ideas or sections of material; asterisks, arrows, bullets, flourishes, etc., can be very effective in organizing large amounts of copy.

• Use an image that shocks, startles or amuses to get your viewers interested in what you're trying to convey.

• Use an image very large, to make the viewer psychologically "back away," or use it very small to make the viewer come closer.

• Combining unlikely images can make a visual "phrase," like a pictogram.

Powerful Visuals

The illustration of a row of dancers on this simple but sophisticated invitation conveys the excitement of an exhibition of the designer's work. The invitation was printed on leftover stock from another print job; creative use of screens gives the illusion of more than two colors.

P O R T R A I T S

Large, beautifully shot black-and-white "portraits" of zoo animals provide an arresting visual indication of the Cincinnati Zoo's highest priority. A second color, red, is used sparingly to draw the viewer's attention to the smaller photo and caption.

MARGAY
(FELIS WEIDII)

HIGH IN THE CANOPY OF THE SOUTH AMERICAN RAIN FOREST, THE MARGAY LEAPS AND CLIMBS THROUGH THE TREES, LIKE A TRAPEZE ARTIST PLAYING TO AN AUDIENCE. THIS LITTLE CREATURE IS ONE OF THE MOST AGILE AMONG THE CATS. ITS FEET ARE MUCH WIDER AND MORE FLEXIBLE THAN THOSE OF ITS RELATIVES, AND IT HAS THE ABILITY TO ROTATE ITS HIND FEET A FULL 180 DEGREES. WITH LONG STEELY CLAWS, THE MARGAY IS A FORMIDABLE ADVERSARY. WHEN IT COMES OUT AT NIGHT TO HUNT, IT HAS ITS CHOICE OF MANY SMALL ANIMALS.

NEEDLESS TO SAY, SCIENTISTS HAVE A HARD TIME KEEPING UP WITH THE MARGAY TO STUDY IT IN THE WILD. AS A RESULT, LITTLE IS KNOWN ABOUT THE CAT'S HABITS. WHAT WE DO KNOW, HOWEVER, IS THAT SOME HUMANS HAVE MANAGED TO CATCH UP WITH THE ELUSIVE CREATURE. THE MARGAY'S SLEEK COAT CAN BE FOUND IN FURS ALL OVER THE WORLD. RECENTLY, TOUGHER INTERNATIONAL CONTROLS HAVE RESTRICTED THE FUR TRADE, PROTECTING THE BEAUTIFUL YELLOW AND BLACK COAT OF THE MARGAY. YET, IT MAY NOT BE ENOUGH. LOSS OF HABITAT CONTINUES TO THREATEN THE LITTLE CAT, LEAVING THE ACROBAT NO PLACE TO CLIMB AND LEAP.

The zookeepers call her Little Girl. This beautiful margay was still considered a kitten when she was rescued by the Fish and Wildlife Department. She was being smuggled in the trunk of a car over the Mexican border in Brownsville, Texas. Now, she's almost old enough to have kittens of her own.

When Pat Callahan was growing up he had unusual domestic animals as pets. Now he has an exotic cat in his care that can be friendly and playful one moment, aloof and mischievous the next. He says it keeps him on his toes.

Powerful Visuals

This postcard uses an effective visual/verbal analogy between a type treatment of the word "commotion" and an archival photo of a volcano. The piece is printed in three colors on inexpensive stock.

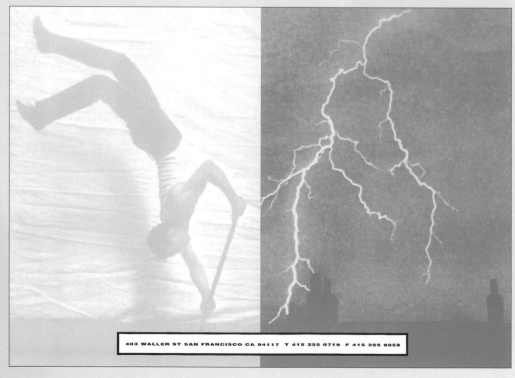

403 WALLER ST SAN FRANCISCO CA 94117 T 415 255 0719 F 415 255 8058

Creating Great Designs on a Limited Budget

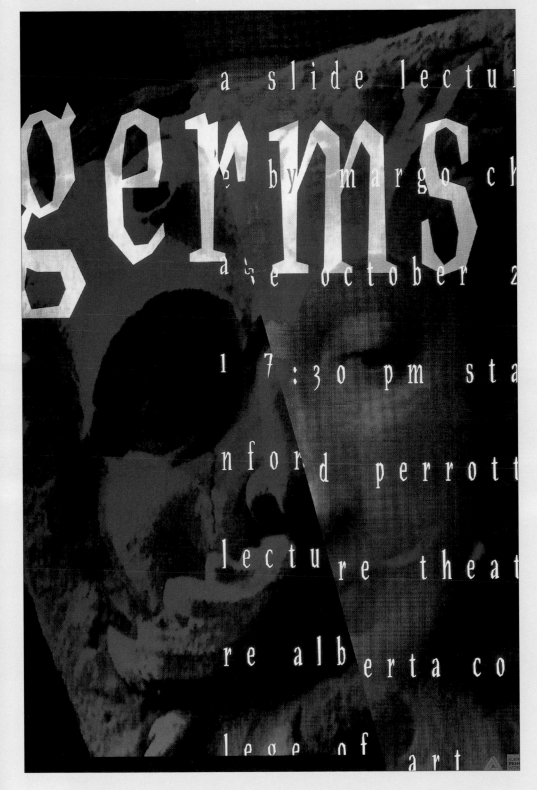

By using only type and two photographs in the public domain, the designer created a complex image. Scanning an existing halftone created a controlled moiré pattern on the image of the Mona Lisa. Another strong image is created with the use of a two-color duotone on the photo of the classical sculpture.

Simplify, Simplify

The key issue in producing any design piece at low cost is simplicity. Keeping your concept simple will allow you to communicate powerfully without breaking the bank; keeping the execution simple, too, will save you time—and time is money.

In keeping things simple, remember the most essential design principle: unity. Relating all elements to each other—all words and images working together to send one message—creates harmony and strength. Begin with a basic image—a large single visual or a powerful headline—and build your design around it. Be sure to use ample white space. This helps to organize the component parts and provides breathing room for the eye; it also helps to draw attention to an important visual or headline. Use bulleted copy lists or subheadings to group related elements. This reduces the total elements to a manageable number and simplifies the message for your reader.

Try to use only what's essential to communicate your message. Carefully consider each visual's purpose and only use those that are necessary; if you have two mediocre pictures and one good one, it's often better to print the good one large and cut the other two. This will add strength to your piece, as well as cut down on cost.

Likewise, try to limit the number of typefaces and sizes you use. Too many different typefaces in too many different sizes can be confusing to the reader and can give a disorganized look to your piece. And while some designers can successfully integrate many faces and scales in a single piece, a great deal of experience is required to do this well. So a good

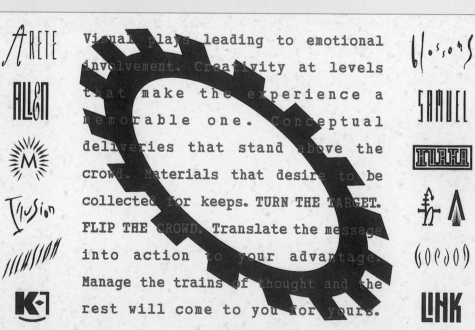

This self-promotional postcard is a great example of keeping the format simple. Where other designers create elaborate booklets to show off their logo work, this postcard shows off Segura's logo work just as well, and at much lower cost. The postcard is a simple two-color printing job that is enhanced by the use of a uniquely textured paper stock.

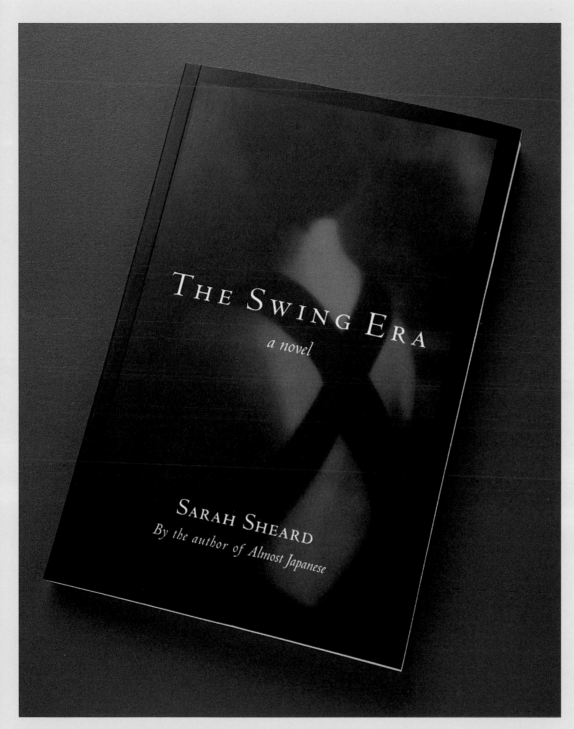

A lush duotone with a classic type treatment reversed out of it gives this piece
an opulent look that belies the simplicity of its design.

Simplify, Simplify

rule to follow, particularly for beginning designers, is to select no more than a few fonts and point sizes per piece. If you're working on a computer, this will save you time in production, particularly if you change your mind about type style or size, since it will make it quicker for you to reselect and change your type. For designers who use a typesetting service to generate type, using fewer fonts will also save on cost.

Keeping things simple also means limiting the number of screens or tints you use. Don't fall into the common trap of trying to stretch dollars and create "color" by using a selected ink at 10 percent, 30 percent, 60 percent and full strength. This often makes the finished piece look cheap, not colorful. And unless you're using a computer, screens usually cost between fifteen and twenty dollars in most markets, and by using three or four you can easily nickel and dime your way to higher production costs.

Instead, use colors at full strength in limited quantities rather than using screens at all. Maybe set a masthead or headline in a bold solid color, then print a flat tint of the same color behind a halftone. This may have more of an impact than dozens of screened areas and boxes used throughout the piece.

Another way to achieve simplicity is to evaluate the format of your piece carefully to determine the simplest and cheapest format you can use to effectively communicate your message. Is a four-color brochure necessary to the success of the piece, or can your message be communicated just as effectively with a postcard or two-color piece? Simplifying formats, whenever appropriate, will make

In this self-promotional piece, each logo gets its own separate sheet, and the minimum of copy and graphics and the subtle use of the second color ensures that nothing distracts the viewer's attention from the logos. The pages were ganged together on one press sheet, then trimmed; a die-cut folder in two colors and varnish holds the pages together.

A clever logo applied with a rubber stamp to a one-color print job gets all the attention on this simple stationery system. The designer kept things simple and avoided the obvious by varying the color within the system by changing the paper, not the ink on the rubber stamp.

your project both cheaper and quicker to do, as well as giving additional weight to your message.

To simplify your designs:

• Use a single visual very large—this gives the viewer an immediate focal point.

• Make the headline large and isolate it in a sea of white space; keep all other copy and visuals small. Or emphasize a single, strong visual by isolating it in a large amount of white space.

• Avoid using lots of solid color or bleeds on a piece; these elements will raise your printing costs.

• Try using only type if your budget is extremely limited.

• Limit the number of typefaces and graphic elements; it's much easier to organize your design this way, and you can always go back and embellish after the major elements are in place.

• Use colors at full strength in limited quantities rather than lots of screens.

• Keep the grid simple. This will save you time, especially if the grid is to be reused periodically, as in a newsletter. Using a difficult grid will complicate the design process every time you work with it.

Simplify, Simplify

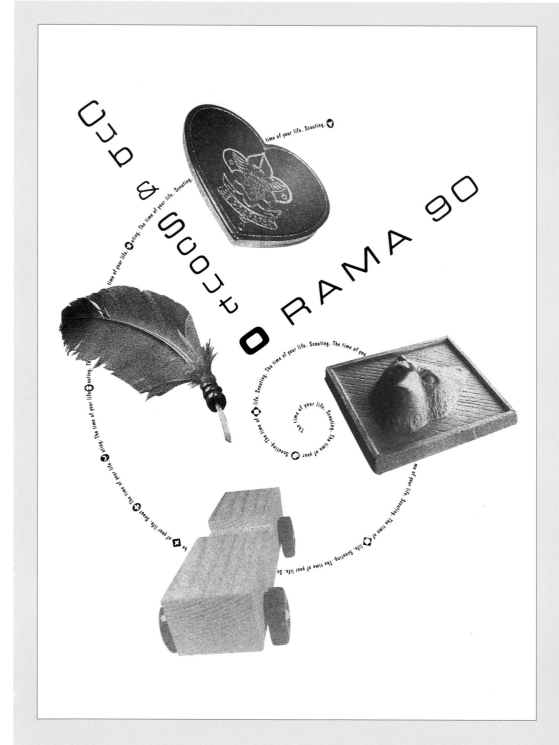

Nostalgic icons of the world of scouting (soapbox car, achievement badge, feather) are used as large, attention-getting images. The "spiral" of copy draws the viewer into the poster.

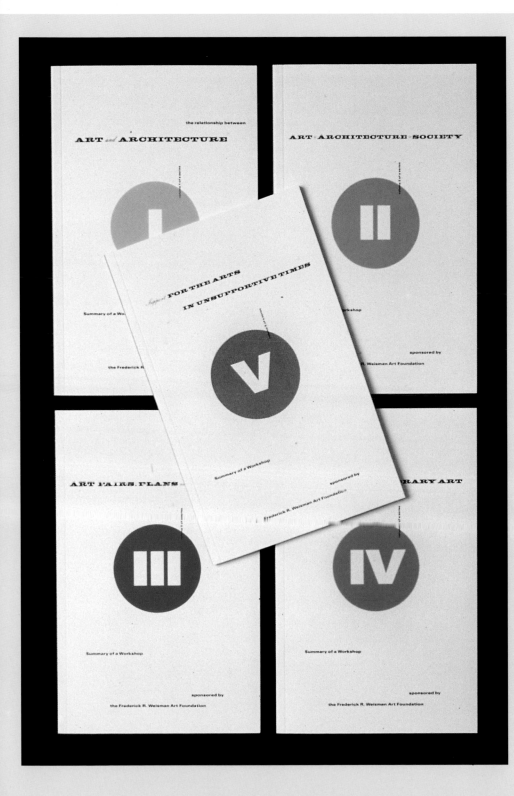

To create a consistent look for the covers of a series of books on varied topics, the designer opted for using a simple graphic treatment of the volume number.

Put All Your Eggs in One

When dealing with a limited budget, it can be wise to commit most of your production dollars to one special design element. There's a tendency to start with a budget of, say, $500 and to spend $100 for paper and $150 for a photograph, and then to evenly divide the rest according to your production needs. But doing this dilutes the strength of your design and, therefore, your message. It's better to do one thing so well that it attracts attention and communicates your message memorably, than to do three or four things that will simply be average.

To accomplish this, reflect on your concept and see if it lends itself to one element that will add distinction to your piece. For example, if your piece focuses on an environmental issue, use recycled or handmade paper. Not only will this work effectively in communicating your message, it will add a tactile element to your piece. However, first consult with your printer to anticipate any special production requirements that can make the job too costly; some papers may be best used for limited print runs. Also keep in mind the possibility of using a unique solid or patterned colored stock, which can also expand your design options dramatically.

An expressive photograph or illustration—especially a high-quality one—can serve as a powerful visual element in a printed piece and can reinforce your verbal message. The work of a good photographer or illustrator will cost you more than clip art or some other cheap source of visuals, but paying more to obtain high-quality graphics for your piece can be worth the dramatic impact the visual

An inexpensively produced two-color poster becomes a clever use of trompe l'oeil with the addition of a gold foil stamp in the form of a racing emblem.

Creating Great Designs on a Limited Budget

Basket

This Christmas party invitation uses a simple three-dimensional element; by adding a ribbon to hold it together, the designer has taken it past the usual flat, conventional invitation and turned it into a gift package.

You are cordially invited to attend the Europe Group Christmas Party at Moraine Farm on Thursday, December 10, 1992.

Cocktails at 7:30 p.m.
Dinner at 8:15 p.m.

$12 per person

RSVP to
>
by Monday,
November 23

will make and the emotional tone it will create.

While clear varnish doesn't change the color it covers, it does give sparkle to it. As an additional bonus for pieces that are handled a great deal (such as business cards or catalogs), varnish will prevent fingerprinting, smudging and scuffing that may detract from your piece's overall appearance. Varnish can also be used to cover selected portions of a printed page; this is called spot varnish. Spot varnish can be used to create subtle background patterns and effects; the combination of matte unvarnished areas and shiny varnished areas can provide subtle visual interest. Spot varnish can also be limited to photographs or illustrations to provide additional emphasis to the visuals.

The use of a foil stamp can also add interest to a one- or two-color piece. The rich metallic look can add luxury to an otherwise basic design. Embossing also adds both visual and tactile appeal, in a more subtle but equally distinctive fashion. Embossing can be "blind"—that is, done directly on unprinted stock—or it can be done in combination with printed graphics. In either case, the size and location of the stamped or embossed area should be selected in consultation with your printer since costs vary based on these factors.

The physical format of the piece can also dramatically affect the amount of attention it will get. Simply making a piece oversized or uniquely shaped will get attention, but there are other things you can do to make your piece special. For instance, simple graphics can be enhanced tremendously by experimenting with

Put All Your Eggs in One Basket

unusual sizes, folds or shapes. Movable parts that have been die-cut and folded can also add interest to your piece. (A die-cut is made with a shaped blade, cutting a slash or shape into a piece of paper. A die may be expensive to produce, but once made, you own it and can reuse it whenever you need to. Collect dies, then use existing ones in new projects when appropriate; while this feature can add cost, it may also provide the distinctive element you're looking for.)

When you're developing a piece to be mailed, the outside container can be more critical than what's inside, since your first and most important task is to motivate the recipient to look further. Consider the container *before* designing the piece it contains. Envelopes, even unusual ones, generally come in standard sizes. A printer or supplier you know may have an overage on another job that will meet your needs without costing you a small fortune, but if you design the contents first, you may need to redesign your piece to fit within the envelope.

In short, don't scatter your eggs; decide what basket you're going to put them in and work with that in mind.

Some tips for using special elements:

• Use a foil stamp to give an opulent look to an inexpensive piece.

• Use a die-cut to give a unique three-dimensional effect that can be achieved no other way.

• Commission a high-quality illustration or photograph that will draw even more attention than lots of color or fancy stocks.

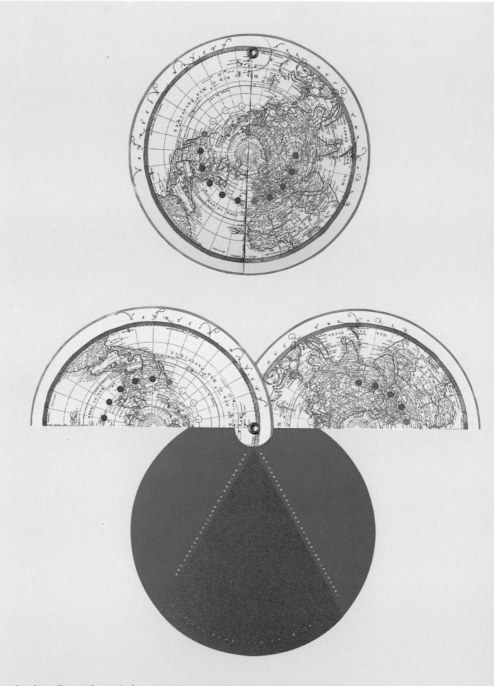

A unique die-cut that swivels open with a grommet gives this simple card extra impact. The graphic of an antique polar projection map with international time zones stresses the international aspects of the institution.

Creating Great Designs on a Limited Budget

- Use spot varnish to highlight certain visuals, or to create subtle background patterns and effects.

- Use a unique binding; spiral binding, for instance, can also expand your design possibilities, as this allows you to mix different stocks and/or colors within a piece.

- Purchase a type font that you haven't seen used too much and build your design around that font.

- Use a colored metallic ink to add an opulent look to a piece. Just keep in mind that to get the most out of a metallic ink, it must be used on coated stock; if used on uncoated stock, the ink sinks into the paper and appears duller.

- Personalize a piece. Plug in the recipient's name on a laser printer or by hand. If you know something about the recipient, add an image that you know will be especially appealing. This technique is particularly effective on a self-promotion piece.

- Use a simple pop-up or hand apply a three-dimensional object. Anything that makes a printed piece more tactile will draw extra attention.

A simple eight-page, two-color booklet is given a special look by the cover it's sewn into. The cover's blind emboss, the richness of the paper, and the rustic stick closure makes an impressive presentation. Much of the work on this piece was done by hand, a viable technique only when producing small quantities.

Put All Your Eggs in One Basket

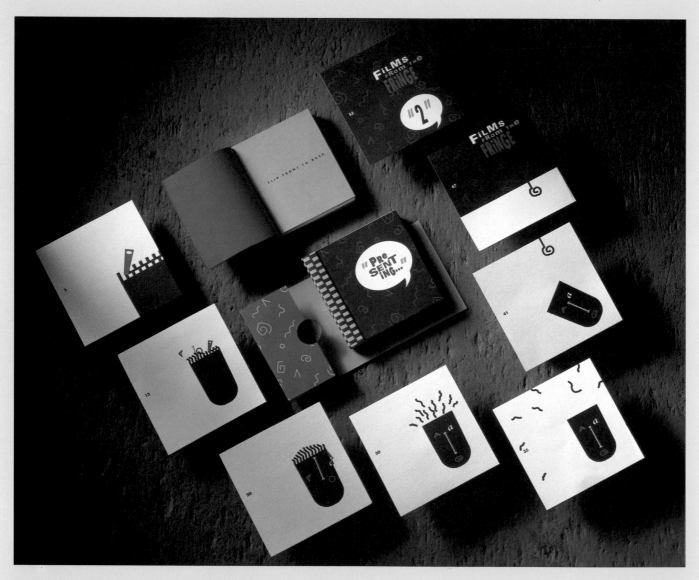

A simple three-color design and illustrative style is brought to an animated flip book announcing the showing of a series of films. The printing and production costs were kept to a minimum to produce the multi-page booklet with a somewhat expensive binding.

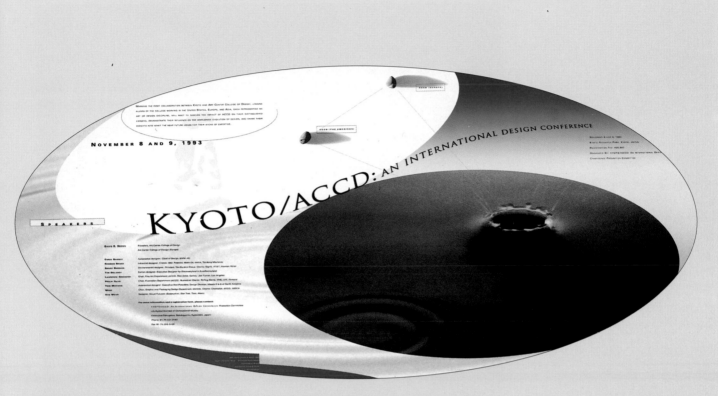

A unique die-cut shape and superb photography make this piece much more
than the sum of its individual parts.

Contrast Attracts

One of the most effective design principles is contrast. The juxtaposition of two seemingly different elements, contrast engages the reader by breaking through the perceptual screen. It helps the designer achieve maximum impact in the delivery of the message.

Contrast can be created in a variety of ways. One way is to vary the scale and weight of type and images. Using very large images next to very small ones, or dark, bold shapes with pale or translucent ones, will allow you to achieve this effect. By using a block of small type that looks gray next to some large bold copy or a headline that looks black, you can create contrasting "colors." Or, you can give weight to only a few words by using bold or caps to highlight important copy. The use of reverse type can also create a dramatic effect. Designing facing pages to mirror each other—one black with white type, one white with black type—can effectively provide contrast too. Contrast can also be created by using negative space to call attention to an important element like an illustration or headline.

You can use color to create contrast too. But this doesn't mean that you must bear the expense of additional colors. Even if you're only using two colors, contrast can be achieved by using a warm and a cool color together. Try an outlined halftone over a warm pink next to a halftone printed over a cool green. A splash of one vivid color in a sea of black and white can also be effective.

Contrast can also be created by combining different shapes and angles, for instance, combining italic and roman type. The use of dissimilar forms also generates visual

Alternating black-and-white pages are brought to life with accents of bright green and cartoonish illustrations. The various typefaces and sizes also work to create contrast.

Creating Great Designs on a Limited Budget

Developing a conviction about a work of art is a very personal process that begins in fits and starts. When the first impression comes like a slap or like a caress – you are probably looking at art. However, we all know to distrust first impressions.

There are certain photographs by Leeanne Schmidt that have an electric sensuality that jolts the viewer into high alertness. First impressions are followed by questions: "What am I looking at?" "Why does this look human?" "Are the curves and goose pimples of human skin really so elegant?" "Where does the peculiar vision of the camera stop and the sensible, visible reality of the body begin?" "How does the beauty of the body revealed here correspond to inherited, learned, advertised or instinctual senses of beauty?" "What distorting and yet amplifying effects are made by the water?"

For me, the more questions, the better the art. The number of avenues leading into, and out from, a work of art is the essential issue. I am little concerned about what the art represents, or what answers it holds. Rather, I want to see what questions are raised: visual, verbal, political, sexual, artistic, racial, photographic, psychological, personal. Many questions elicit many answers.

I find in these photographs questions of beauty colliding with a queasiness about the grotesque. The rippling water, unfamiliar angles and oddly conjoined parts, can erode and yet also accentuate what is beautiful and what is grotesque in each body. These photographs explore the stark divide between the two categories of experience: not entirely placid, nor fearful – not simply ravishing, nor repulsing. There is something of Mapplethorpe in the photographs but also of Matisse and Renoir, celebrating and re-celebrating the continuous perceptual dance between models and artist. Drawn into the photograph by the comfortable, inviting familiarity of the human body, the approach gives way to a quaking ambivalence of perceptions as the viewer works to locate, identify, re-synthesize the beautiful ambiguous parts into a new sensual wholeness of figurative beauty.

The slap of first recognition and the multi-phased perception of these photographs has firmed my conviction that Leeanne Schmidt is up to something fresh, energizing and new. See what you feel

Jack Sawyer 6.30.93
Former Curator
The Contemporary Arts Center, Cincinnati

For me, water is a metaphor for emotions and feelings.

Just as the water moves, so do our emotions.

– LEEANNE SCHMIDT

Sparse and restrained use of typography and lots of white space
make the photograph zoom out at the viewer.

Contrast Attracts

A secure environment for your records

Your documents are protected by a sophisticated fire and security alarm. Smoke detectors, heat detectors, sprinkler system and intrusion devices provide an extremely secure environment.

The warehouse is monitored 24 hours a day, 7 days a week by a U.L. approved central station.

For security purposes, only authorized individuals with a valid password are allowed to request documents. In addition, only Off-Site employees physically handle the documents.

SECURITY

24 Hrs.

MONTGOMERY WARD & Co. CHICAGO.

Within the pages of this large-scale booklet, contrast is created by the varying scales of type and images and the juxtaposition of a vibrant yellow with good old black and white. The designer used simply drawn artwork along with old line art to keep production costs to a minimum.

A grid of stark type blocks and rich duotones creates strong contrasts. There is also a "rhythm" created by the lines underlining the text type and the lines in the furniture that is being shown. The duotones create such an illusion of depth when juxtaposed with the flat blocks of copy that this becomes yet another form of contrast.

intrigue—juxtaposing fluid, free-form shapes with geometric or rigid ones is effective.

Try using patterns or textures to create contrast. Some computer software can produce patterns quickly and easily. If you don't have access to a computer, similar effects can be achieved with Zipitone, old wallpaper, other found objects, or photographs of patterns and textures like stones, bricks, grass or the sky.

One last word on contrast. Not only should your design include the element of contrast itself, the finished piece should contrast with the pieces with which it must compete. Before developing your design, take a careful look at what your competitors are doing. Create something different that will stand out and grab viewer attention.

Ways to create contrast:

- Use a light typeface for text and a bold face for captions or vice versa.

- Mix serif and sans serif typefaces within a word or phrase.

- Mix sizes of typefaces within a word or phrase.

- Pair a headline set in small type with a large photo or vice versa.

- Juxtapose areas of contrasting colors—for instance, combine a dark version of a cool color and a bright version of a warm color.

- Trap an area of bright color in an area of solid black.

- Put a page with a busy illustration or a busy type treatment opposite a page with a lot of white space.

The Element of Surprise

When something conflicts sharply with our visual expectations, we give it more attention than something we're prepared to see. The unexpected causes us to do a double take, looking the second time more closely and with greater interest. Your printed piece will receive much more attention if you include an element that surprises your readers. In the same way that movies can keep us on the edge of our seats anticipating what's to come, printed pieces can include suspense that keeps us involved and wanting to read further. Longer pieces, such as booklets, can sustain interest by using this tactic.

One way to create surprise is to use unexpected visual images. Photographs, illustrations or other graphics that are in clear contrast to your verbal message stimulate interest. Images that poke fun or serve as visual puns are also highly effective. Communicators have been using humor to convey messages for hundreds of years. The only caveat here is to make sure that what *you* think is clever or amusing elicits the same response from your target audience; if there's any doubt, seek a second (or maybe a third and fourth) opinion. This tactic works most effectively for a piece with a short shelf life, since humor loses its surprise appeal with repeated exposure.

Surprise can also be achieved with unexpected color. Both in nature and within our culture, we associate certain objects with certain colors. Use of a color or colors that conflict with reality or our expectations can often cause viewers to look again.

Unexpected papers can also be interesting. Try using a translucent

The combination of old advertising art and hand-drawn antlers that mimic the original style results in this eye-catching and surreal logo for a restaurant.

The viewer is surprised twice by this memorable holiday card: first, by the startling photograph—an atypical choice in itself for the holiday season—on the card's front, then by the card's punchline.

This holiday season, save a turkey!

Put another shrimp on the barbie, mate.

The Element of Surprise

paper for an unconventional, see-through effect. Unusually shaped photographs can also be intriguing. If the subject matter permits, cut your photos in the shapes of letters or objects relating to your message.

One of the most effective ways to add the element of surprise to a design is to manipulate its physical form in an unexpected way. Pieces that have been assembled by hand—that have a hand-stitched binding or a hand-cut closing—are captivating. Pieces that have been drilled, burned, ripped, riveted or otherwise altered will also catch the receiver's attention.

The addition of a three-dimensional element to your otherwise two-dimensional piece will also set your design apart and bring more interest to your message. Including objects found in nature—like twigs or pine needles—is an inexpensive way to add a tactile element and to expand the involvement of the senses in the piece; there are plenty of other objects you could consider that don't cost much, such as nuts and bolts, sandpaper, balloons or party favors, or buttons or Velcro. These objects can be used to either reinforce or satirize your verbal message.

A word of caution, however, on incorporating hand-done elements into your design: while they are highly effective in attracting attention and in making your piece both distinctive and memorable, they should be used only when a piece will be produced in limited quantities. If you are able to do the handwork yourself, or have access to a small group of volunteers who will help out, the results can be terrific. But if high numbers require that you pay for hand work, it may

The inclusion of an inexpensive plastic toy magnifying glass in this party invitation for *Spy* magazine makes a clever, and unexpected, visual pun.

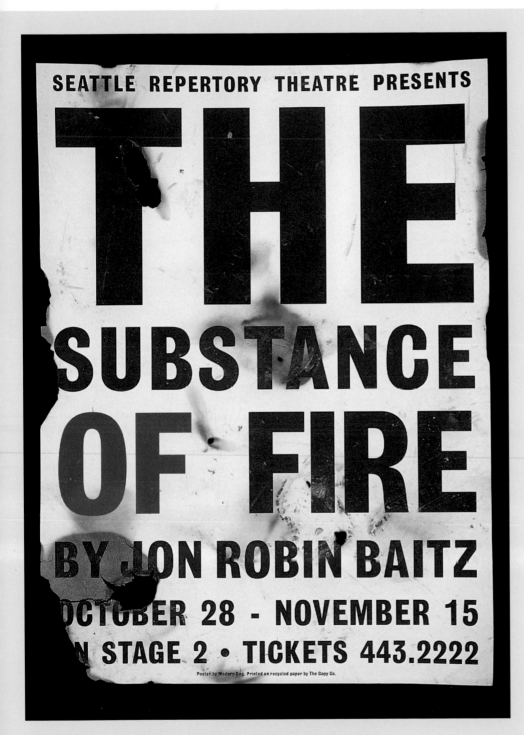

Areas of this poster were burned by hand, surprising reinforcement of the title of
the play that the poster promotes. Only two hundred of the posters were produced,
making it possible for this handwork to be done quickly with cigarette lighters.
The poster was printed in two colors on inexpensive stock.

add significantly to your production costs.

Another caution: Remember that an unpleasant surprise is counterproductive if you hope for a positive response to your message. Think twice before filling up an envelope with glitter or sand and sending it to anyone. Try to put yourself in the shoes of the recipient—is this a surprise you would want to receive? If the answer is no, then think again.

More ideas for incorporating surprise into your designs:

• Contrast the headline with the visual—for instance, "cold" with an image of flames.

• Use a visual pun with an appropriate headline.

• For a brochure or booklet, use a simple headline on the front page that leads recipients to expect one thing, then surprise them with an unexpected first spread; or continue the opening headline in an unexpected way on the first spread.

• Begin a mini-booklet with cryptic images, then, only on the final page, relate the images to the subject.

• Use a format that's unusual. Some formats—such as flipbooks or pop-up cards—are unusual in and of themselves; other formats can be unusual for the subject they cover—such as using a newsletter to promote a product or using postcards instead of a booklet as a catalog.

The Element of Surprise

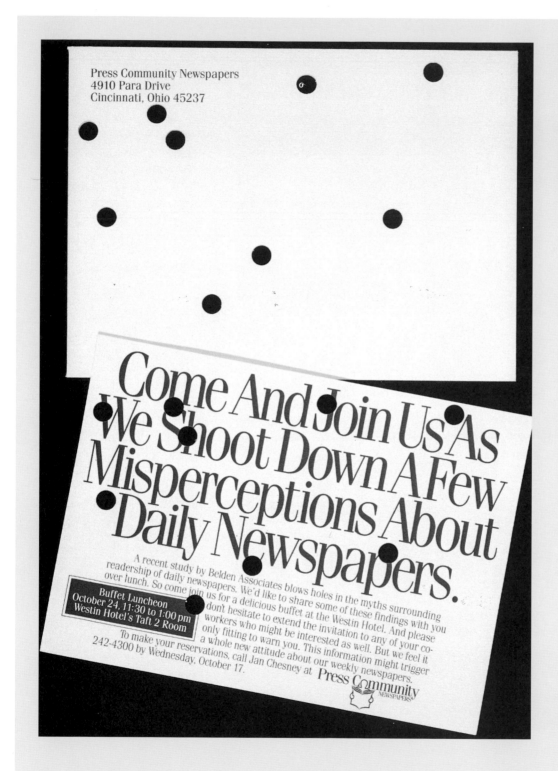

If you got a piece of mail with a number of holes drilled through it, wouldn't you open it? This piece uses these holes—created simultaneously on the mailer and envelope with a drill punch—to play on the piece's "shoot down a few misperceptions" tag line.

Creating Great Designs on a Limited Budget

The audience expects lots of words or visuals on the first few pages of a gallery catalog, so this piece is quite a surprise. The first three spreads simply finish the name of the exhibition, "Drawing into the '90's," one word at a time.

Following Through

As you conceptualize your printed piece, keep in mind that the elements you choose to incorporate must work in harmony with one another. It's critical that the type and visuals you select, the paper you choose and the physical format of the piece follow through with the message. Each of the elements that you use plays a part in creating the whole, and each should contribute to the effectiveness of your message. Including a clever die cut or tactile element that has nothing to do with the theme you're trying to create will distract the reader from your intended message. Select and incorporate only those elements that contribute to what you're trying to say.

"Following through" also means looking at the big picture—meaning that if you're working on a series of pieces, or a brochure or poster that's part of a larger communications campaign, consider the pieces as components of a single message, and make sure they work well together. By repeating the same type styles, the same colors, and some of the same images, you'll ensure that your message is clear and consistent. You'll also get more mileage out of each individual piece, since each one will be a thematic or visual reinforcement of the pieces that come before or after.

In addition to following through conceptually, it's important to follow through on the production of your piece. Craftsmanship and attention to detail are critical to the success of any graphic communications piece. Have you ever seen a great brochure in a terrible envelope? Or a wonderfully designed poster that was mailed folded, creasing the headline? How about a piece with carefully selected

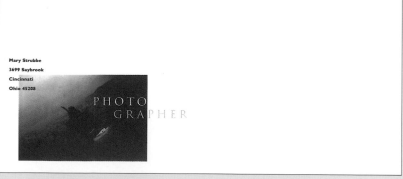

Even though different photographic images are used on each component of this stationery suite, color and typography are consistent, giving all pieces a family look.

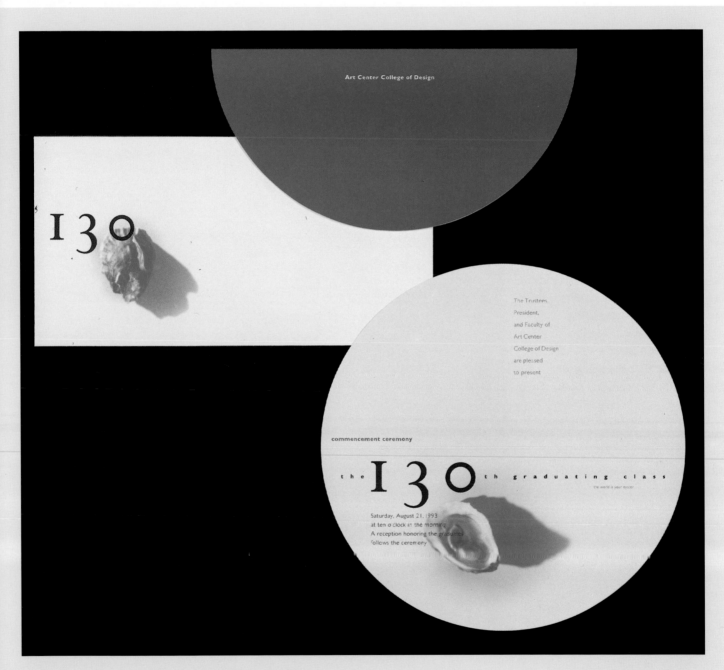

This die-cut invitation is beautifully thought through and coordinated. Consistent typography, image and color is used on both pieces to give the receiver a "complete" message.

Following Through

colors printed on a paper that didn't allow their brilliance to come through? Designers of these kinds of pieces don't understand the importance of following through.

To be effective, a piece must be produced carefully and with close attention to every detail from conception through delivery. This is especially important when working with a limited budget. Limited resources don't allow for mistakes that require the reprinting of brochures or the reordering of envelopes. A good way to ensure that this doesn't happen is to lay all the ground work first. Start by figuring out what the hardest thing to get will be, then work around it. If you've found a great envelope, find out what sizes are available and double check postal size and weight requirements before designing and printing the piece that goes inside. Or, if you're designing a logo or identity package, make sure the logo works well in a variety of sizes and colors and can be reproduced on different surfaces. Logos can appear on anything from business cards to billboards. Anticipating this at the design stage rather than dealing with alterations or redesign later will make your life much easier in the long run.

Always keep in mind that poor execution will undermine even the strongest of ideas.

Ask yourself these questions to make sure you're carrying a consistent theme throughout a piece:

• Does every portion of the piece, even the envelope, convey the same message? Even though the envelope for an invitation or announcement is usually discarded, it's the first thing

The designer of this invitation booklet followed through in a number of important ways. First, to get the piece noticed in a stack of mail, he picked a stock red envelope, and then designed the booklet with both the color and the size of the envelope in mind. Second, he used the piece's two colors consistently throughout the booklet—even down to putting the red accent color to use in a map at the booklet's end. Finally, the reply and order cards pick up the design of the rest of the piece.

Creating Great Designs on a Limited Budget

viewers see, and therefore your first opportunity to get them interested in your message.

- Is a particular part, material or element difficult to find? If so, make sure you can obtain it before you plan your design around it.

- If you're doing a series of pieces, are the look and tone of the pieces consistent throughout the campaign? This can be achieved through using a common image, color or typeface.

- Is there a commonality between the cover of your brochure and the inside pages? The pages of a piece need not be identical, but there should be some element that ties them together visually.

Each part of this announcement-within-an-announcement is related by the use of common colors and materials—all of which in turn reinforce the message of this piece. Pockets inside each piece hold pine needles, sunflower seeds and bird seed to reinforce the messages inside. Each folder is held together by a piece of raffia and affixed with a sticker.

Chapter Two

The Power of Limited-Color Design

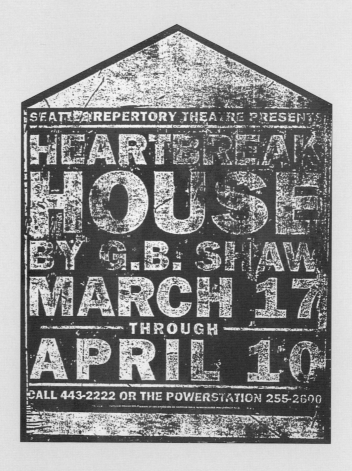

Working with limited color is one of the most common ways to save money in design. But having to do so doesn't spark joy in the hearts of most designers. Who wouldn't rather have every color combination in the world to work with? But in a culture where over-the-top visuals are routine, even top designers with hefty budgets have learned that careful utilization of the starkness and simplicity of one- and two-color design is likely to make their pieces stand out from the crowd.

There are practical advantages to designing with fewer colors, too. Beyond just being a cheaper print job, quality of the print job will be easier to control, and the job will likely be printed faster. And fewer colors will generally mean quicker production on your end.

There is a downside, however: the design of a limited-color piece must be good, since no gimmicks will camouflage any flaws. Remember the advice in chapter one: Begin with a good idea, then pare it down to its essence. And then, learn what the limited-color designer's best friends are—type, photography, abstract graphics and line art—and how to use them to their best advantage. You'll save money on printing and production. But more importantly, you'll be on your way to effective communication.

Learn how to make the most of the multiple possibilities of one- and two-color design.

Typography as Art

Just as good writing clarifies a verbal message, effective typography clarifies a visual message. For designers with computers, typography is the easiest design element to experiment with. Hit a few keys on your keyboard and you can change your primary font; hit a few more and you can undo what you just tried. With this technological ease, there's no excuse for a designer who works on a computer not to make the most of type.

However, before you get too carried away with the possibilities of type, educate yourself about type design theory. Learn how to really see type, so you can use the strengths of each typeface, and each kind of type treatment, to its best advantage.

For instance, on close examination, you'll find that each typeface has a specific personality that you can use to help communicate your message. Serif type is generally considered more classic, while sans serif type is considered more contemporary, or even high-tech. Within these two categories, there are thousands of typefaces, each having a distinctive shape and personality. You can choose a typeface that is appropriate to the tone of your message, or you can create visual interest by selecting a face that contrasts with your message.

Also consider the size and weight of the type you've chosen. Large, bold type conveys more importance than small, light type; italic type tells the reader to pay closer attention. Using a size or weight that confounds the viewer's expectations is another way of catching attention, and of making type work for you.

The arrangement of type is equally important—it shows readers

Bulletin

1993   1994

Cleveland Institute of Art

Using just the letter *b* from the word "bulletin" this designer created a striking catalog cover. The letterform bleeds off the four sides of the page to create dynamic positive/negative space.

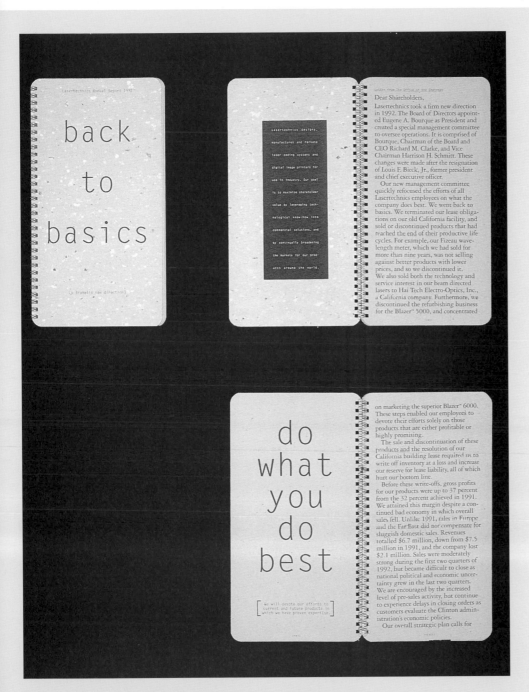

In this annual report, printed in black ink on various shades of earthtone paper stock, type is used to achieve "tone." Large headlines, copy reversed out of black rectangles, and blocks of text are the three elements that produce a "rhythm" within the piece. Wire spiral binding was used so the various colors of paper could be placed wherever the designer chose.

where to begin, affects when and where they pause, and determines what parts of the message receive serious consideration. Justifying copy, or setting it flush right or left, subtly conveys various degrees of rigidity or fluidity. Various widths of leading (the space between lines of type) also convey different moods: Copy with wide leading usually suggests luxury, while copy with narrow leading conveys the opposite (and, of course, copy with no leading or that overlaps with the line above it is now the cutting edge). Also try imaginative arrangements—such as rotating or skewing type, or setting it in wavy lines or in a circle—to draw attention to short blocks of copy.

Reverse type—white type that appears on a black or colored background—can also be very powerful, drawing attention to a word or words by creating value contrast. Because of its dramatic appearance, reverse type effectively highlights critical copy or quotations. Take care, however, to pick type that will reverse out well; with small type or type with thin lines or uneven serifs, narrow areas may fill in when printed.

When used well, type can be powerful enough to justify a type-only design. You may choose this route when there are no illustrations or photographs appropriate to your message or when you want to save on the cost of using such graphics. And sometimes words can be more powerful than images, allowing the viewer to conjure up his or her own personal interpretation.

Fortunately, as well as being one of the most effective design elements you have at your disposal, typefaces are also among the least expensive to have and to use. At twenty-five to

Typography as Art

eighty dollars, a single typeface can expand your design choices immeasurably; having a flexible and well-chosen typeface library is crucial. Since you probably can't afford to buy every typeface you like, it's important to choose your fonts wisely. Your computer probably came with many of the classics pre-installed; choosing additional typefaces depends on your (and your clients') taste. Build your typeface wardrobe as you'd build your clothing wardrobe—start with classics and add trendier pieces cautiously.

As a low-budget alternative to buying trendy display typefaces, design your own unique display type. There are many software programs to make type generation and manipulation easy; among the most popular are Aldus PageMaker, Adobe Illustrator, QuarkXPress and Typestyler. These and others will allow you to create or change the size, weight and shape of a wide variety of typographic forms. Or try manipulating a typeface by hand, either by embellishing it or cutting and pasting it back together; experiment with distortion on a photocopier. Or hand letter or stencil type to create the desired mood.

Whatever you do, keep in mind that your message is still paramount. Never manipulate important copy at the expense of readability.

Ways to use typography as a primary design element:

• Use a single, large letterform as a starting point for your design.

• Use various sizes of type to reinforce your message (for example, large type=loud, small type=quiet); or to get attention, confound the

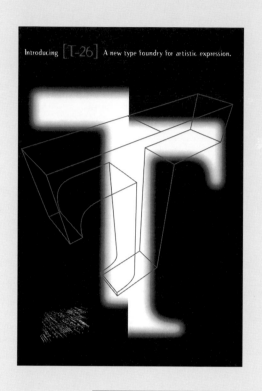

Cover and pages from a type font catalog show no limit to creativity in terms of layout. The catalog's auxiliary copy is as creatively designed as the typefaces themselves. Pages were presented loose in a cloth bag to save the cost of binding, and printed on a high-quality laser printer so they could be produced as needed.

Here type is used to form an image in which the information is contained. Letterforms are skewed, curved and stacked vertically to make the shapes needed to form the image. Artwork was duplicated and offset for the second color to achieve a shadow effect.

reader's expectations by making unimportant words or phrases large, and important words or phrases small.

• Manipulate type by hand or with the computer—stretch, condense, distort, expand it.

• Mix contrasting typefaces within a single headline, or even within one key word.

• Use a typeface that contrasts with the mood, look or theme of the piece for a key design element; using a playful face on a serious piece can add interest through contrast alone.

• Use hand-lettering or handwriting to set a mood. A child's crayon lettering might work well for a piece on day care; elegantly handwritten headlines might lend a sense of warmth and humanity to a health center brochure.

• Reverse type out of circles, ovals, rules, boxes and other shapes.

• Wrap blocks of type or lines of curved type around an image.

• Give lines of type motion by curving them into "waves" or making them radiate from a center point.

• Use initial or drop caps to spice up unbroken text.

Typography as Art

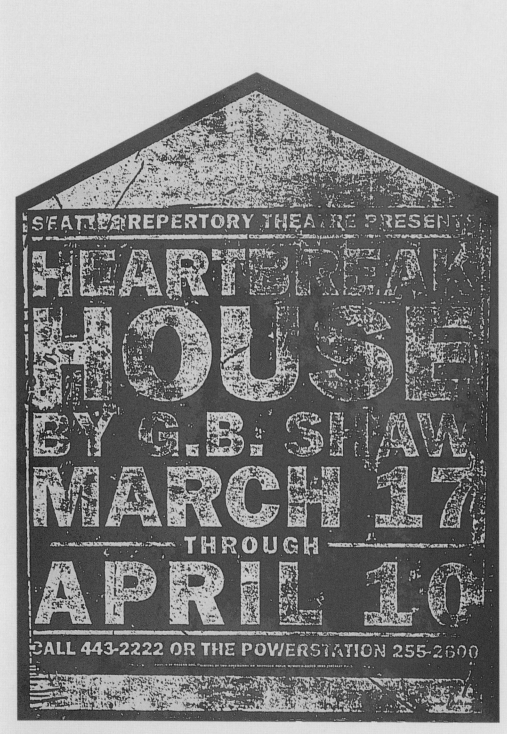

This simple, all-type design is made unique by the hand manipulation of the type to look old and weathered. The poster was silkscreened and then trimmed at two angles on top to suggest the shape of a house.

Hand-lettering, various computer typefaces and enlarged typewriter type are mixed together to give an idea of the diversity of the work in the exhibition being promoted. The piece is printed in black ink on white stock to avoid letting color confuse the message; designing the piece to be printed on one side only helped keep costs down.

Using Photography for

As we all know, a picture is worth a thousand words. And technological advances have revolutionized the use of photography in design. Scanners, for instance, have made photos cheaper to use. It's no longer necessary for designers to rely on printers to shoot film and translate photographs into halftones; a scanner can do it in the design studio. Software programs such as Adobe Photoshop are also having a tremendous impact on how designers can electronically manipulate photographs—even designers who don't draw can create photo-illustrations cheaply.

Despite this revolution, there are a number of constraints in the use of photography in design, especially for those with a limited budget. You'll still need to consider the quality and reproducibility of your photographs as well as what to do when they don't pass muster. In judging which photo to use in a piece, you'll still need to consider which will reproduce properly. Photos with good contrast, or those that can be reprinted to improve contrast, are generally best.

If your photograph passes this initial test and also has excellent content and composition, you may want to use it as the focal point of your design. But it's more likely, especially if you're working on a low-budget project, that you'll have to work with a photo that's less than ideal. Fortunately, there are many inexpensive techniques to help you maximize whatever photos you have. For instance, if your photo's problem is a lack of contrast, this can be adjusted for little cost with image manipulation software such as Adobe Photoshop or Ofoto; your printer can do this if you don't have the software.

The designer used a "found" photograph, in this case a publicity still from the film, and added his own line work to allude to Wittgenstein's golden mean. The photograph is cropped close in, to bring the viewer into the subject matter. The poster is printed in navy blue ink, to give the photograph and typography strength and mystery.

Maximum Impact

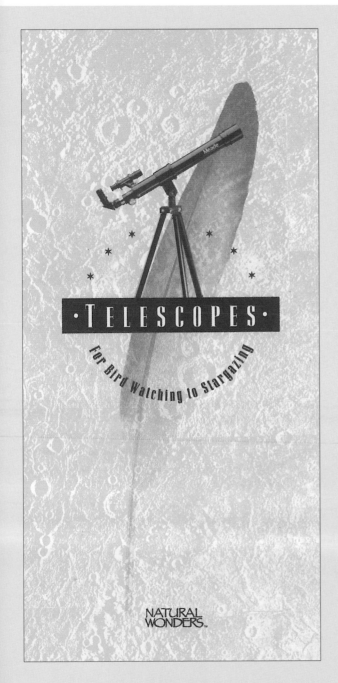

·TELESCOPES·

For Bird Watching to Stargazing

NATURAL WONDERS™

To visually represent the tag line "For Bird Watching to Stargazing", the image on the cover of this brochure is made up of three photographs that have been overlapped and silhouetted. The background is a "ghosted" photograph of the surface of the moon, over which has been placed a photograph of a bird's feather and a photo of a telescope. The feather and moon surface photos were "found" images, and the photo of the telescope is a product shot from the vendor. High-volume, one-color printing made the per-piece price very low, but wise use of subtle duotones and textured paper gives the piece an elegant feel.

You can use this same software to apply filters to alter the photo's appearance, allowing you to improve contrast or even turn photos into line art.

If your photograph is blurry, you might consider blurring or distorting it further, both to communicate action or turmoil, and to hide its flaws. As always, only use this technique if it's consistent with your message.

If your photograph is dull, try unusual cropping to add interest. Cutting off unlikely portions and using the fragments throughout your piece can intrigue the viewer. Or try very tight cropping to bring more attention to the photo's subject, or skewed or asymmetrical cropping for drama. Photographs cropped into shapes or letterforms can add interest. This is an especially useful way of dealing with boring "head shots"; just be sure to keep the feel of the entire piece in mind before getting too creative.

To hide flaws or to create a mood try varying your line screen. A coarse line screen will create a comic book effect, while a fine line screen will create a more detailed look. Or you can use a high contrast scan (called posterization) or a photocopier to convert your photo to line art and give it the look of realistic illustration; this will also save the cost of having a halftone made.

Duotones are another inexpensive way to add impact to your photos. A duotone is a two-color halftone that is made from a black-and-white photograph. The photo is actually shot twice at different angles, once for the first color, usually black, and once for the second color; the combination of halftone dots from the two plates creates a complete range of tones. Not

Using Photography for Maximum

only are duotones visually effective, with Pantone's Color and Black Selector 1000 you'll be able to see how the final effect will appear. The cost of a duotone is roughly twice the cost of a one-color halftone, since the printer will have to shoot two pieces of film instead of one and since a second color will be used.

You can also use photographs to provide texture for your piece. A photograph of a repeated pattern can add visual interest when used as a background beneath type or other images. A ghost halftone—a photograph screened back to subtly stand behind type or other images—can also create an interesting background effect. However, this element must be handled carefully and in consultation with your printer so as not to overshadow your copy and dilute the strength of your message.

One last point: However you incorporate photographs into your pieces, make sure you have written permission to use them, even if they've been supplied by your client. If the photographer or owner of the photograph requires it, credit him or her in your piece. If rights to the photograph you want to use are in question, you may be better off finding another or taking one yourself; preventing a lawsuit is the easiest way to avoid breaking your budget.

To use photographs for maximum impact:

- Make photos more dramatic by cropping or by making them very large or very small.

- Alter your photos with various line screens to achieve more or less detail.

This photographic stationery system features a silhouetted duotone of a stone, suggesting that a single stone can be the starting point for a landscape design. Each piece of the system has a different color of stone to add interest to the system when all the pieces are viewed together, and to keep costs low.

Impact

The designer superimposed type over a strong close-up photograph of a woman's face to result in an intriguing cover for a book of poetry. In some areas the type is darker than the background, in some places lighter, almost as if the designer is giving us a glimpse of the woman's thoughts. Printing this photograph as a black and brown duotone gives the image a warm, sensual feel.

- Use posterization, steel etch and mezzotint—camera processes that turn photographs into line art—to achieve a "look" and eliminate the cost of halftones.

- "Ghost" a halftone to create a background pattern.

- Reverse out type or print type over photos.

- Place a photo inside or overlapping a letterform.

- Take a black-and-white photograph and hand tint it with markers or special tinting paints to create an old-fashioned effect or to draw attention to one particular element in the photo.

- Use duotones to give bland photos extra visual impact; for instance, try combining black and a sepia tone ink in a duotone to get a period effect.

- Keep in mind the kind of paper you plan to use, and pick your photographs accordingly. Remember that uncoated paper such as newsprint tends to bleed more and photos will usually print darker on it. Coated paper allows the dots of ink to sit on the surface of the stock, and as a result, photographs don't bleed as much and will appear somewhat lighter.

Using Photography for Maximum

 In writing, God *(and sometimes the devil)* is in the words and in the way words are crafted together; every scribo should tell himself every morning,

IT'S THE STYLE, STUPID.

Photography can be used in a highly imaginative way to illustrate a potentially dry topic, as proved by this booklet promoting the services of a technical writer. The designer took photographs and manipulated them with Adobe Photoshop to come up with these surreal photo-illustrations.

is each of them not just important but essential? . . . *is every last word* SHAPED, *cut, turned, ground, and* POLISHED *so as to* EXPOSE *and* CLARIFY, *with exacting tolerances, the ideas the writing is intended to* *impart to readers?* . . . but without boring those readers?

Which leads to our second proposed standard for evaluating scribo's work product, reading theory.

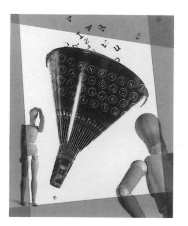

Impact

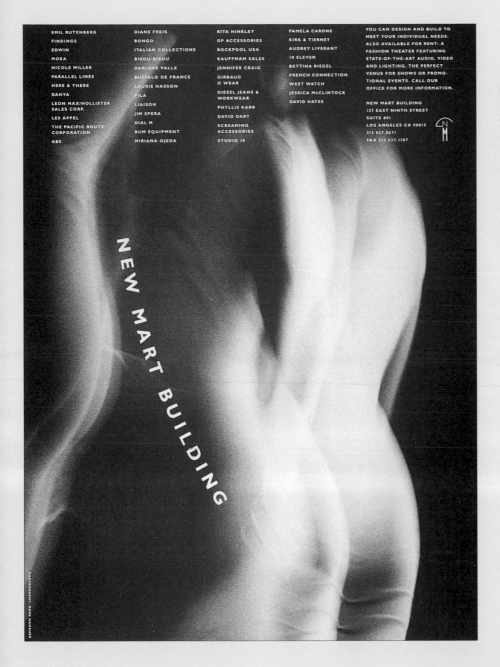

This advertisement for a high fashion designer's center uses a black-and-white strobe photograph as its visual centerpiece; action and excitement is implied by the somewhat blurred photograph of a female form in a simple dress, but the photographer is careful not to show a particular piece of clothing. The type and logo are reversed out of the dark areas in the photograph.

Using Abstract Graphics

One of the best ways to keep costs down on a printed piece is to use abstract graphics, such as lines, boxes, screens and shapes, instead of photographs or illustrations; abstract graphics are both readily available and easy to create, and they stand up well even to the cheapest printing processes. If your budget is limited, learn to make the most of these often overlooked or misused graphic elements.

Abstract forms can create visual interest, especially when color is used to make the images and their relationships even more striking. Shapes, in particular, can be useful for dividing your space visually— creating positive and negative areas—and for giving life to the page.

Abstract graphics can also be used to organize copy on a page. Rules, boxes and screens can visually compartmentalize information, helping the reader move through the message more easily. Shadow boxes can add a three-dimensional look to a piece while emphasizing blocks of copy. A lines or a series of lines can draw the reader's attention to headlines or subheadings.

While we usually think of abstract graphics as creating a contemporary feeling, they can also be used to create a more traditional look. Small Victorian patterns or prints and marbleized textures and borders can create a period tone while organizing copy on the page.

And don't forget ethnic and historical patterns, such as African, Egyptian or Native American patterns, or even early American quilt patterns; many designers rely on trips to art museums and a library of art books to help educate and inspire

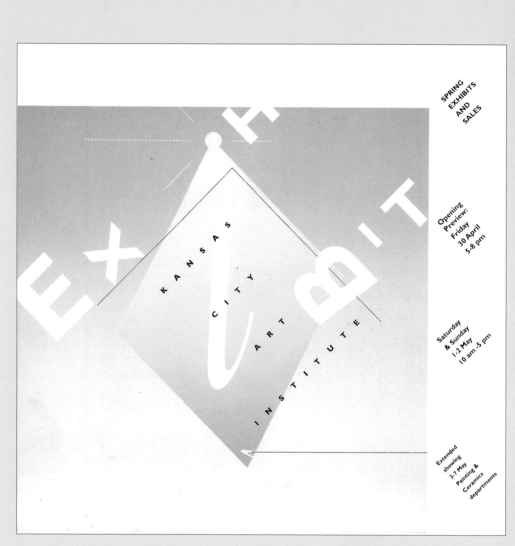

Gradation blends created by Aldus FreeHand, reversed and surprint type, and rules are the three elements used to create this highly "kinetic," yet graphically simple design.

Using only dark gray ink, both at full strength and screened to several percentages, the designer created a visually complex piece. A found image of an eye and a photocopy of a ruler are the starting points for this catalog cover for a graphics course. The inside of the catalog is also one color and was designed to be easily updated.

Using Abstract Graphics

them in the creation of contemporary versions of traditional patterns.

Whatever kind of abstract graphics you decide to use, they're among the most readily available of design elements. Many simple abstract images are available through any basic layout program. More complicated shapes can easily be drawn in almost any software program. The real beauty of using abstract images is that they're easily drawn by hand, even if you don't have much experience drawing; you can then scan in your pattern and clean it up in your software program, or you can use it as finished art.

Dingbat fonts are also readily available to those with computers. Once you've bought the font—and the cost of one of these fonts is generally no higher than the cost of a typeface—the images and symbols can be incorporated into your designs at no additional cost and can add significantly to your message. When repeated or combined, dingbats can also be used as ornamental rules, patterns or textures. One good, inexpensive source of this software is Image Club Graphics, Inc., in Milwaukee, which offers fonts, digital clip art, and even photo design elements through their catalog for as little as fifteen to twenty dollars each. Check out graphic design magazines for advertisements for both well-known and obscure companies selling all types of fonts. In the past, dingbat fonts were almost always completely copyright-free; however, some of the newer ones are now copyrighted, so don't assume something is copyright-free without checking.

Finally, remember that all graphics carry with them certain feelings

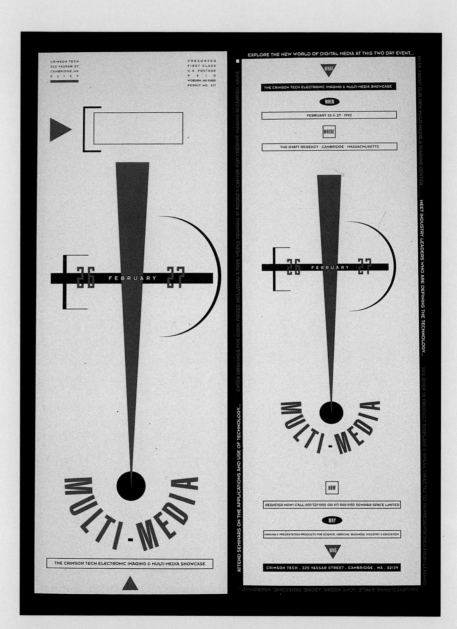

Simple graphic devices—parentheses, exclamation marks and brackets—combine to make an active image for a poster announcing a multimedia trade show. This simplicity is especially effective for this promotion—since multimedia products and conferences are often promoted with very elaborate visuals printed in many colors, the simplicity of this piece makes it stand out from the competition. Printing the piece in two colors on colored stock gives it the look of a three-color piece; the simplicity of the entire design ensured that the posters could be produced on a tight schedule.

Simple graphics such as a bullseye, arrows and a human skull convey to viewers what this poster is about before they read the copy. The images, the angular hand-drawn type, and black ink on brown kraft paper work together to give the piece drama and urgency.

or moods, and using them in your designs will communicate those feelings to your audience. As with any other design element, be aware of the emotional connotations of the abstract graphics you intend to use.

To incorporate abstract graphics into your own designs:

• Use screens, such as drop shadows, behind lettering or images to create depth.

• Use rules, ruled boxes and screens to organize information.

• Use a repeat pattern to activate and unify a page.

• Create patterns and textures with a photocopier or scanner from fabric, wood veneer, textured or marbled paper, bark or rice paper.

• Use gradations, created either with Pantone gradation paper or on the computer, to give depth and "light" to a piece.

• Use picture or dingbat fonts; enlarge them as a focal point of your design, or use them to emphasize important information in your copy.

• Use a mathematical pi font— which produces a variety of interesting symbols—as a decorative element; the thick and thin forms it generates can add interesting visual variety to your piece. The forms can be used as an abstract design element or can be built on to create something new.

• "Draw" or produce patterns using only the letters or symbols on your computer keyboard.

Using Abstract Graphics

Using a computer illustration program, the designer created this simple abstract image for the cover of *Emigre*, a magazine devoted to typography, graphic design and music. The image was created using simple abstract shapes and a modified version of a typeface called "Out West."

Once we received the grant, it was time to roll up our sleeves and get to work...We began by asking

QUESTIONS:

"THE MOST EXCITING PART IS
LEAPING OVER ORGANIZATIONAL
BARRIERS. BARRIERS FALL AWAY
How do we build a meaningful Partnership in a county of this diverse population and vast size?
AS PEOPLE MEET FACE TO FACE."
How do we design a different kind of organization, one that involves participation and consensus at
— SCHOOL DISTRICT GRANTS
every step? How can we reach diverse segments of this vast county and sustain their involvement?
COORDINATOR
How can we be responsive to community needs? ✱ These questions reflect the tremendous
challenge of this grant. Traditionally, prevention efforts have been funded for
isolated, "quick-fix" activities and strategies. Instead, the five-year Partnership grant supports our
county to do long-term, community-wide *planning*—and do it right. The Partnership
has also been funded to develop a prevention system that builds *community*
know-how. As a demonstration grant, the Community Partnership will put new
ideas from prevention research into *practice*, and be a model from which promising
strategies can be replicated in other communities. ✱ This is an *innovative*
approach to prevention--bringing people together to work on common causes--
which the federal government is supporting through 251 Community Partnerships nationwide. This
new vision means breaking through barriers that keep people fragmented. Using resources more
effectively. Modeling *participation and consensus* every
step of the way. ✱ It's a complex process that, in a county of this size and diversity, takes time and
"IN MY PROFESSION, IT'S
FRIGHTENING TO SEE THE
thought. It takes the best expertise and guidance from all sectors of the community. It takes a
INCREASE IN VIOLENCE AND
commitment to research and development for careful, strategic planning *before action.* ✱ We took
ASIAN-RELATED CRIME. THE
this first funded year, then, to develop the fundamentals.* To clearly define our role in the complex
DETERIORATION OF PEOPLE IN
marketplace of prevention. To set in motion our direction for the future.
THE PARTNERSHIP GIVES ME
The grant funding pattern set our first year from October '91-July '92. Our second year began August '92.
MOTIVATION TO GO OUT AND
DO MY JOB." — POLICE OFFICER

{ 2 }

THE PARTNERS: It's one thing to bring together *diverse groups and individuals* to plan for
prevention. It's another to find a common-understanding of how to do it. Creating this collective
"I SEE THE PARTNERSHIP AS A
vision was a critical first step for the Partnership. ✱ In the fall, a group of partners attended a
PLACE TO WORK TOGETHER ON
CSAP Basic Community Partnership Institute in Monterey, CA. This workshop introduced the
COMMON CONCERNS, TO HAVE A
fundamentals of developing a Community Partnership. Next we held a working session retreat at
COMMON DEFINITION OF PRE-
Asilomar, CA, with a participant list completely generated by the community. The 84 participants
VENTION." — FAMILY COUNSELOR
engaged in 2 1/2 days of coalition-building exercises, and by the conclusion of the retreat had
drafted this *shared vision* statement:

We will develop a comprehensive system in
Santa Clara County in which our shared
sense of responsibility drives a collab-
orative effort to prevent social problems
and promote healthy communities.

Throughout the year, partners always found ways to be involved in the Community Partnership.
From attending monthly meetings, to dropping by the office with feedback or ideas, their *ongoing*
participation helped guide this first year.
"THE PARTNERSHIP IS ABOUT

LINKING POWERFUL RESOURCES
THE TRANSITION TEAM: A group of people from our original grant steering committee agreed
TO HELP EMPOWER INDIVIDUALS.
to operate as a transitional leadership team. This Transition Team spent six months developing a
THE GREATEST OBSTACLE TO A
governance structure for the Community Partnership. Guided by ongoing input and consensus
PERSON STEMS HELD IN INTRA-
from partners and staff, the Team designed a governance structure that truly reflects Partnership
AGENCY FRAGMENTATION, AND
values, and that provides for different levels of participation by a broad spectrum of people. A work-
THE PARTNERSHIP REDUCES
ing group then continued the process by outlining the kind of leadership the Partnership would have.
THAT." — HIGH SCHOOL ASSISTANT

PRINCIPAL

{ 3 }

Simple abstract shapes, used as a screened background for pages that are
heavy on words, can excite viewers and get them to read the copy.

Working With Low-Cost

Using line art rather than photographs can offer a variety of advantages. First, no halftones are needed, which usually results in lower production costs, especially if you're relying on a commercial printer rather than your own scanner to create halftones. Line art is also easier for a printer to reproduce than photographs, so you can communicate your intended message more effectively, even if you don't have the budget for high-quality printing.

Apart from the practical benefits of incorporating line art, there are aesthetic benefits as well. For instance, if your goal is to create a piece with a contemporary or high-tech look, line art creates this feeling better than a photograph. Line art, such as charts and graphs, can complement narratives and provide a visual break for the eye. In a glance, they communicate change over time and can simplify complicated descriptions and messages. These kinds of graphics are especially appropriate for use in annual reports, financial presentations and demographic charts. The computer software program Adobe Illustrator is the most popular software program for creating charts and graphs, but you can also create them with simple sketches or cut paper collages.

Illustrations used as line art can give your piece added communication power. They offer you an often powerful creative alternative when no appropriate photograph is available. Illustrations can be straightforward and communicate in images what the copy is saying. Or they can be used to expand upon the words and bring the emotional involvement of the reader to a new height. Since

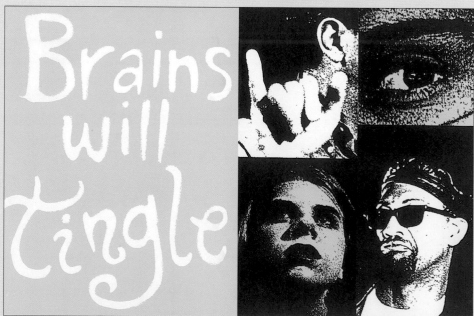

Publicity photographs have been transformed into line art with a photocopier; cropping the art idiosyncratically, and printing the brochure in black and an offbeat green match ink, gives the brochure a cutting-edge look.

Line Art

Our Garden Variety Is Anything But Common. ❧ Come immerse yourself in the magnificent beauty and luscious fragrances of spring. At the Cincinnati Zoo and Botanical Garden's Spring Floral Festival. Mosey through a myriad of gardens bursting with vivid spring hues from a quarter million blooms, exotic plants and historic trees. Gaze upon a lush landscape of flowering crabapples. Pansies. Forget-me-nots. Primroses. Plus, over ninety varieties of daffodils. Tour our European Garden at your leisure. Where weekends a brass quartet fills the air with classical music. And French mimes engage a crowd with their antics. Experience the serenity of our new Oriental Garden adorned with elegant Oriental flowers, plants and shrubs. Where Japanese Koi swim about a quiet pool. And where beautiful plants are available for purchase in our Botanical Center.

SPRING·FLORAL·FESTIVAL·APRIL 13·MAY 12
CINCINNATI ZOO AND BOTANICAL GARDEN
PRESENTED BY THE KROGER FLORAL SHOPPE

Then, visit the Children's Zoo for an unforgettable journey into "The Land of Oz." Where Dorothy and her Oz friends delight children with special weekend events. Today, children are invited to take part in our Earth Day celebration, featuring conservation tips presented by the Oz characters. So join us for the Fifth Annual Spring Floral Festival. And see it in full bloom. Today's Spring Festivities: Earth Day Weekend ❧ Conservation Tips from Dorothy and Oz Characters, 12:30 and 2:00 at the Children's Zoo ❧ Recycling Puppet Show, 2:00 and 4.00 at the Education Building ❧ Conservation Exhibits all day. Next Weekend's Festivities: Heart, Brain & Courage Scavenger Hunt with Oz Characters ❧ Special thanks to WWEZ and WKRC-TV.

Victorian patterns and floral line cuts combine with a modern type treatment and layout to produce this contemporary-looking advertisement. The simplicity of the illustrations ensures the ad will look great, even when printed in the newspaper. Since no illustration or photography was needed, production costs were kept low.

Working With Low-Cost Line Art

illustrations are interpretations, not replications, of reality, they allow you added flexibility in determining the tone of your piece. You can use them to set a whimsical, lighthearted tone or to add an element of humor to a piece, or you can use them to create a dark or serious mood.

If either rendering or commissioning an illustration is not possible for you, several good sources of copyright-free illustrations exist. Among them are the Dover Pictorial Archive Series. This source of illustrations, woodcuts, architectural elements, ornamentation, and folk and African art provides a variety of images that can enhance your piece significantly, and is available both in paperback and on computer disk. Other sources of line art include ARROglyphs; the ClickArt Studio Series; and the Letraset Library. Keep in mind that, even though most of this art is copyright-free, some restrictions may exist, such as limitations on the number of pieces of art used in one piece of design. Check the copyright page—or, if the art is on disk, carefully read any auxiliary material that comes with the disk. Make sure anything you plan is legal.

Ways to incorporate line art effectively into your designs:

• To achieve a rough-hewn look, enlarge small line art to gigantic proportions.

• Transform copy into charts and graphs to communicate better and to add visual interest; for instance, for a newsletter, turn a listing of company events into a timeline or a calendar.

• Use scratchboard illustration to create an earthy, rough, primitive or

A design using bold and roughly hand-cut type minimizes the negative effects of flexography, a somewhat primitive printing process used to print three-dimensional objects and paper bags. Since this printing process is rough, the design doesn't use subtle lines and halftone screens.

highly stylized look.

- Use black ink in dry- and wet-brush illustration to create a fluid or sketchy look.

- Add your unique stamp to computer clip art by adding to, altering or manipulating it to create exactly the illustration you need or the look you want for a project.

- Use conventional clip art images in unusual or surprising ways, such as combining two or more in a collage, splicing together elements from a few pieces of clip art, or adding your own hand-drawn touches to them.

- Use simple line drawings done by children to create a free and fresh tone. In most cases, kids or their parents will simply want to have the work credited in the finished piece.

Antique line cuts, line art and photographs are collaged to create a new image. Printed in black and red on tan paper, this poster has an antique, yet fresh, look.

Working With Low-Cost Line Art

Existing '40s ad cuts have been manipulated and customized to suit this studio's needs. Transformed into low-cost rubber stamps, the images can be used on mailings and interoffice paperwork. Different colors of ink pads add interest to office form papers and envelopes that would otherwise be ho-hum.

An old engraving of a piece of classic sculpture is an ideal image for this
brochure about facial reconstructive surgery.

Chapter Three
Inexpensive
Visuals

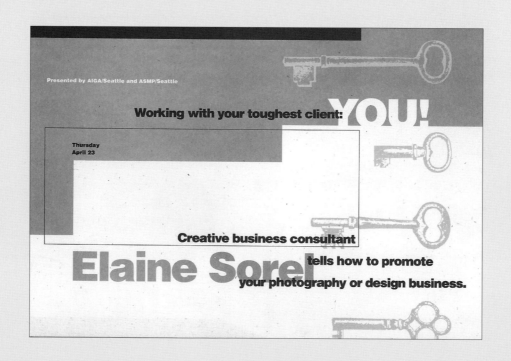

Great visuals need not be costly; there are plenty of ways to save on costs without cutting corners. First, consider the needs of the project at hand; does it really require high quality photography or a top illustrator? If not, use that to your advantage—minimize your use of visuals, or try an all-type design. But if your project calls for lots of high-caliber visuals (a travel brochure, for instance), you'll need to work smarter; find inexpensive visuals or learn how to create them.

Keep in mind that inexpensive visuals may turn out to be costly—both to your reputation and your client's—if they're inadequate or inappropriate. If you can create effective photographs or illustrations, or can find someone to do so inexpensively, by all means do; but try to be objective about whether these visuals are working. This also goes for "found" visuals—just because Victorian line art is cheap doesn't mean that it is appropriate for every piece you design.

Learn how to visualize your message for your audience.

Examine each visual carefully before incorporating it into your design. Is it appropriate for the piece you're designing? Does it fit in well with the other elements? If it fails any of these tests, no matter how cheap your visual happens to be, you're better off without it.

Found Visuals

Great visuals need not be expensive; in addition to clip art, old or outdated published materials can offer an abundant source of copyright-free images. Old newspapers and magazines offer a variety of line drawings, photographs and interesting typographical configurations to enhance your designs; old photographs and postcards can be great sources too. Vintage catalogs, such as a one hundred-year-old copy of the Sears & Roebuck catalog, can also be interesting sources of images. Check out flea markets, thrift stores and used bookstores for such publications; for materials you can use for inspiration (but which you probably won't be allowed to photocopy), go to a library or to your local historical society. Even better, search your own attic; if appropriate to your theme, you could even use old family photographs in a self-promotional piece.

As you look through sources, you may come across images that trigger an idea consistent with the tone you're trying to set or the message you're trying to convey. These images can be used in their original form if they work well with the theme or message you're trying to develop. And don't rule them out if you don't find exactly what you're looking for; these visuals can be altered in a variety of ways with a photocopier, scanner or even by hand. So experiment with visuals and use them to your best advantage.

Take note, however: If you plan to use "found" art as anything more than inspiration, you'll first need to learn the basics of copyright law. Litigation has made using found visuals riskier than it used to be. Copyright law is too complex to sum up here in

A combination of found photos converted to line art, found line cuts, and scanned three-dimensional objects make up the human form "collage" that is the focal point for this poster publicizing an exhibition about industrial design, visual communication and architecture.

Old line cuts of wheels and cogs are used as the main visual in this stationery suite. Printed in light gray, the images function as a sort of "shadow" that can be typed or written over.

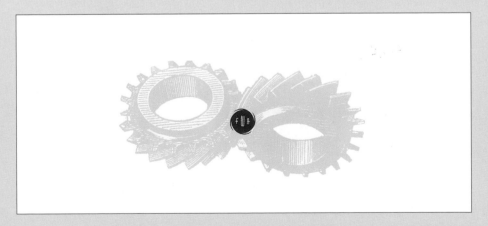

Found Visuals

a few words; for the basics, see *Make It Legal,* by Lee Wilson (North Light Books), or contact the Copyright Office, Library of Congress, Washington DC 20559, (202)707-3000. Generally, works published or copyrighted more than seventy-five years ago are copyright-free; however, it's still possible that a renewal registration has extended the copyright. When in doubt, you'll need to do some research to make sure the image you want to use is in the public domain (copyright-free).

To do this, you'll need to start by examining the work itself for a copyright notice; if you don't see one, you'll either have to make a search of Copyright Office catalogs and records, or ask the Copyright Office to make the search for you. For a search, you'll need the title of the work in which the visual appears, the name of the author or artist, the year of publication, and any copyright data listed. You'll be billed per hour for the search. If the Copyright Office can't find a registration, that doesn't necessarily mean that the piece is copyright-free (there are many variables that could affect whether or not they can find a copyright registration), but you're probably safe to go ahead and use the visual. Make sure to keep documentation of your search, in case the status of the piece is ever called into question; proof that you made a good faith search for the copyright holder should indemnify you of damages, if the copyright holder ever turns up.

It can be difficult to avoid risk entirely when using found art, and the larger the audience for your piece, the greater your risk. Obviously, you probably won't have to do a copyright

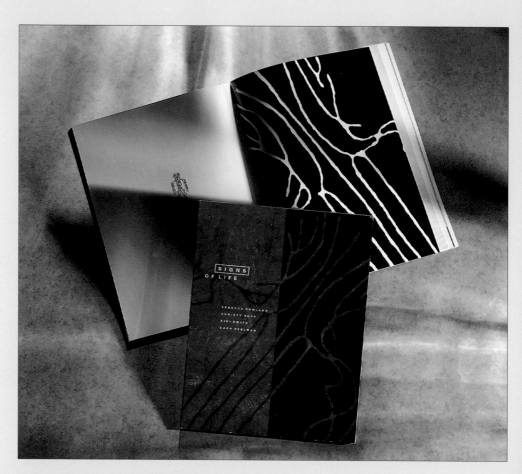

The striking image used on the cover and introductory pages of a gallery catalog about four female figurative artists is, cleverly, an extreme enlargement of a small drawing by one of the artists.

Creating Great Designs on a Limited Budget

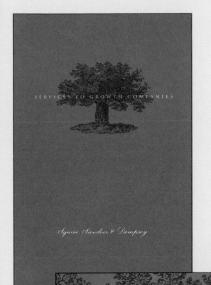

Found in a catalog of clip art, a woodcut of a tree serves as the sole visual in this brochure for a law firm seeking more clients that are growth companies. The same piece of art is used in dramatically different scales and crops, appearing at first to be different art on each page. This is an excellent example of getting a lot of mileage out of a single piece of art.

search if you've used found art to spice up a party invitation, and a copyright search is probably adequate if you're doing work for a non-profit organization, but if you're working on a job that will be seen by a larger audience (such as an annual report or packaging) you're probably better off avoiding found art altogether. There's nothing low-budget about a lawsuit.

More ideas for found visuals:

• Use copyright-free line art and photography that is in the public domain.

• Use conventional and computer clip art.

• Turn dingbats and typographic ornaments into spot illustrations or even a main visual.

• Explore attractive clip art collections and picture fonts, available from a number of sources. They make good spot art, can enhance a newsletter nameplate, or otherwise dress up a piece.

• Put three-dimensional objects on the photocopier or flatbed scanner and experiment with creating line art from them.

• Consider rubber stamp artwork to illustrate a variety of subjects.

• Look to graphics used in previously printed pieces for the same client to incorporate into new designs. Not only will this save money, but it will develop continuity in the client's visual identity.

Found Visuals

An eclectic assortment of found line cuts and archival halftones convey the
diversity and excitement of a three-day architects' convention. Color has
been added to the black-and-white line art and halftones to give them more
dimension. The invitation and reminder use some of the same images in different scales, and both pieces were printed simultaneously on a single sheet,
to save on printing costs.

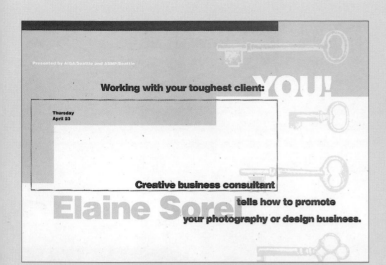

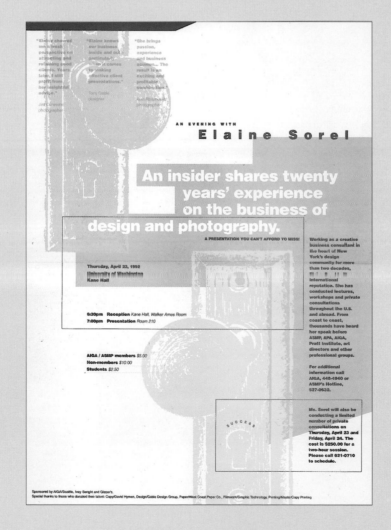

Line cuts of keys and door knobs found in an old hardware catalog are used here as a visual metaphor for seeking knowledge.

Create Your Own Visuals

If you don't have access to, or have decided not to use, any of the sources of existing visuals we've mentioned, there are a number of techniques you can employ to create your own visuals with good results. Each technique carries its own flavor, which will also affect the tone of your design.

The use of basic shapes is an easy way to add visual interest to your piece. Geometric or abstract shapes will create one feeling while representational shapes will create another. Shapes can be hand torn, cut out, or produced with a good deal of accuracy and precision with a computer; choose whichever method is most appropriate to your message.

Incorporating a woodcut, scratchboard or linoleum print in your design can add artistic flair. Even if your piece is two-dimensional, this type of visual adds depth and a tactile quality to your work. In addition, the images you create can be interpretive and extremely effective in emotionally involving your reader. If you've never worked in these media before, they will require a minor investment in materials (such as handtools) and practice. While this type of printmaking usually doesn't require excessive production time, learning the techniques may require more time than the schedule of your project permits. You may want to brush up on these techniques between design projects so you can use printmaking visuals in the future.

The use of hand-drawn illustrations can create interesting effects and add considerable impact to your piece. Illustrations need not be complex to be effective; both pen-and-ink and dry-brush reproduce well and can be done well with practice.

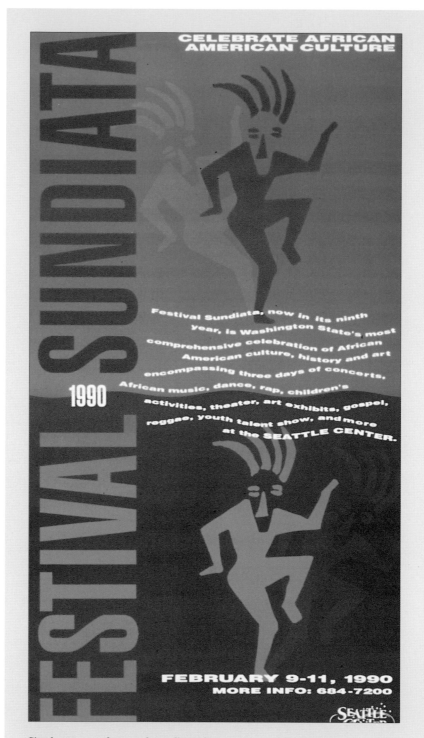

Simple cut paper forms and wavy lines of type get across the excitement of the event this poster is promoting. Two contrasting colors further enhance the excitement. Because the poster is virtually one solid color, the reversed white type appears almost as a third color.

It's for all the kids on the block

SHOOT, GIVE US AN IDEA

This is where the idea started. Every kid loves to shoot hoops. The idea was born. A 10,000 square foot facility with a full-sized gym with courts for kids of every age and every race. Open games on a daily basis. So instead of hanging out on street corners waiting for it to happen—it's always happening at the FreeZone. And it's free for one and all.

WHAT'S THE NET RETURN?

Then we added volleyball to the mix. Volleyball was another great way to build inter-racial cama-raderie and team spirit. Using organized sports to diffuse pent-up energy, adolescent frustration and potential aggression, the FreeZone becomes a safe place for kids to channel emotions in a positive, productive environment.

PLAYING IN UNISON

With the musical enthusiasm of today's youth, the FreeZone will include a whole musical repertoire. In addition to encouraging kids to make their own music, we'll bring the music, offering concerts throughout the year.

IT'S A WHOLE NEW WORLD

The FreeZone. Think of it as a world without boundaries. Kids from different cultures, different ethnic backgrounds, sharing in one free environment. Forget the problems of the past. Think of our future.

The FreeZone's the best idea on the block

A stylized and simply executed illustration of a child playing basketball is the centerpiece of this poster, which announces a youth program designed to keep children out of trouble. Such an illustration could be created easily in an illustration software program, with cut paper, or with freehand drawing.

Create Your Own Visuals

If you have access to a computer and the appropriate software packages, you can create simple art for effective visuals. Software programs such as Adobe Illustrator and Aldus FreeHand allow you to create images and illustrations easily; one advantage to using these programs is that images created on them can be handed to your printer on disk and can go directly to film. You'll avoid the extra cost of high-quality printouts of your art. With some programs, it's also possible to manipulate existing clip art to create your own images with both found and created forms.

If your message lends itself to it, create a collage by combining scraps of construction paper, clip art, old magazines or maps, or even old design projects. A collage can be used as a background pattern, a border, or as a full-fledged illustration, adding life to your design at very little cost.

Common or found two- or three-dimensional objects can be photocopied or scanned and used as interesting visual elements. Try laying type over one of these images to reinforce the words, to pull together type and image.

Try these techniques to create your own visuals:

• Simple illustrations made from cut black paper shapes can make a bold graphic statement, even if the execution is less than perfect.

• Scratchboard, woodcut and linoleum-cut art require a little more finesse to look good, but can make strong visual statements for the right messages. A simple linoleum-cut of a sunburst, printed in gold or orange, could be a perfect image for a poster

Blocks of color combined with simple brush and ink line illustrations are used here to represent specific plays in a series. Although all of the images use the same elements and style, each has its own unique message.

The designer of this piece used a collage of found materials, artfully arranged, to create rustic visuals for the cover of this photographer's portfolio.

The designer of this poster used the traditional image of a chicken as a "taking off" point for the more contemporary version at the bottom of the poster. The illustration was created with a computer illustration program, but could easily have been done with black paper cutouts.

announcing a company's summer picnic.

• Dry-brush and ink illustrations, which have a casual look, can be created with a little practice and add a fun, relaxed feeling to a piece.

• Create art with your computer. Using an illustration program such as Adobe Illustrator or Aldus FreeHand, you can create simple or complex images.

• Create your own maps, charts and graphs where the content lends itself to those treatments; a simple bar graph or pie chart is easy to execute and, if done creatively, can add much visual interest.

• Try your hand at collage with scraps from magazines, old projects, or old maps; simple one- or two-color paper constructions can add a lot to a piece with minimal time and effort.

Create Your Own Visuals

Three type styles, a checkerboard pattern, a stylized leaf, and a grouping of rules was all that was needed to create the visuals for this restaurant packaging.

MULTIPLE *perspectives*

An easy-to-execute brush and ink illustration works well here to illustrate the idea of "multiple perspectives." The designer did several versions of the drawing, then combined the individual elements that worked the best into one illustration. Type is used cleverly as part of the illustration itself.

Getting Photographs

As we've already mentioned, there are a number of advantages to using photographs to add visual interest to your design. Photographs give your message realism and communicate on a powerful emotional level with your target audience. And unlike illustrations, which may need to be commissioned, pre-existing photographs are often available from your client.

If no photos are available and you must hire a photographer to take pictures for use in your piece, look for one willing to exchange a reduced rate for a prominent photo credit and samples of the piece; this means good photographs for you and a portfolio piece for the photographer.

Another option is to take the photos yourself; that way you can determine the exact composition and tone you want. You can decide who will be pictured, and in what context they will appear. Use friends as subjects if you can't afford models. Set your own stage. Be creative.

If your photographs won't be reproduced in full color, take them with black-and-white film. Most printers prefer to work with black-and-white prints in this case and the final results are generally better. The lower the ASA of the film (or speed with which the film uses light to capture the image), the more crisp the images will appear. Film with an ASA of 100 or 200 will produce very sharp prints, while film with an ASA of 400 will produce a more grainy picture. ASA 400 works well for action photos, while ASA 100 or 200 yields greater detail and precision.

If you're planning to photograph people, try to limit the number of individuals in each photo. The fewer

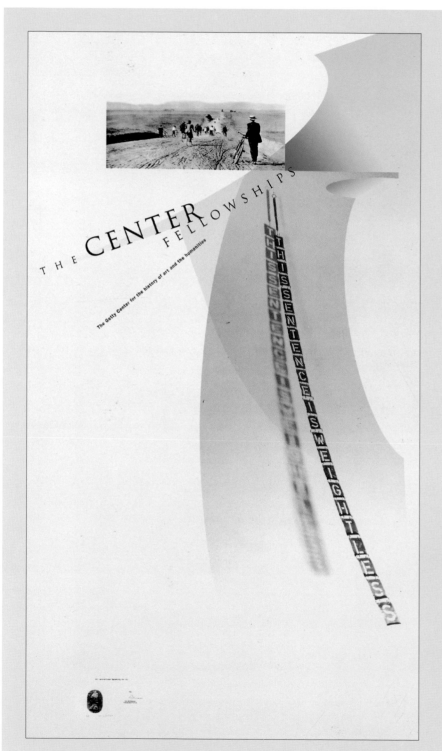

This elegant poster was created by combining a stock archival photograph—which simply conveys the historical mission of the Getty Center—and computer-generated gradations.

Cheaply

Scanning some nails on a flatbed scanner created this "photograph" for the cover of *Greenkeeping* magazine. This issue featured an article on ecologically responsible home design and building. The nails were scanned in such a way as to retain some of the gray scale, and printed in green ink to reflect the environmental nature of the publication.

people pictured, the more involved the viewer can become with each. When possible, try to take candid rather than posed shots. There's nothing more deadly than a posed photograph of a handshake or a check passing. Your photos should be filled with action, emotion or both. Photography can enhance your ability to communicate with real people about real people on an emotional level; use that to your benefit.

Keep in mind that, if your photographs are going to be reproduced in black and white, good contrast is necessary for acceptable reproduction. Make sure your lighting is good. Your subject matter needs a variety of dark and light tones, rather than only middle-range, dark or light tones. If, for instance, you're photographing a gray object to be reproduced in black and white, make sure the background is either very dark or very light; a gray object on a medium-range background will result in poor contrast. The more contrast you create in your shot, the more "readable" it will be and the greater the impact of the photograph in your finished piece.

There are a few advantages to developing pictures yourself, if you have access to a darkroom. While this can be time-consuming, it may still be quicker than sending out film for processing, especially if you're working with black-and-white film. The number of black-and-white photo processors has decreased to the point where it's often hard to find someone who will do a good job processing black-and-white film, and as a result costs can be high. Developing and printing your own black-and-white photos may save you money. If this isn't an option, consider using a local college's

Getting Photographs Cheaply

facility to help with processing.

Processing color photographs is a different story. It's become affordable to have color film processed. Discount photo shops and even some of the "mail away" photo processing services will do a competent job and can even print your photos in a 4 x 6 or 5 x 7 format.

Always remember that photographs don't have to be perfect to be usable. You can employ any of the techniques mentioned on pages 52-57 in chapter two to salvage less than perfect photos (even ones you've taken). However, don't feel obliged to use bad photographs just because you've spent time and money to produce them; cut your losses and write this time and money off as a learning experience—and cut the photos from your piece entirely. Never give up trying to learn new skills, but keep the needs of your piece ahead of the needs of your ego.

Ways to get photographs inexpensively:

• Use stock photos that can be rented for a one-time usage fee. This can be expensive, but depending on the subject matter, location and complexity of the shot, using stock photos can be less expensive than hiring a photographer.

• Create "photographs" on the computer. Computer illustration programs have a "blend" tool that can create gradations from light to dark. Using this in conjunction with the other tools, you can create images that have a "photographic" effect.

• Mix computer art with existing photography.

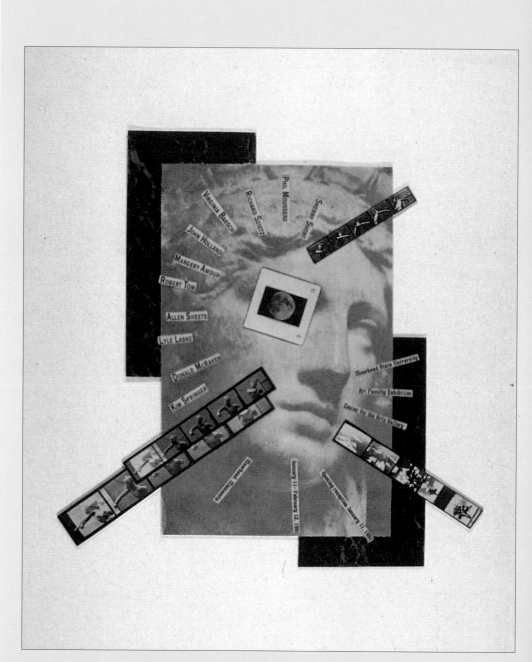

A found photograph of the Statue of Liberty, a 35mm slide, and strips cut from a photo contact sheet make up this image for a faculty art show.

neo-
mania

Nº 24

Price $7.95

The designer took this photograph of a trash can, then silhouetted it on the computer using a photo manipulation program. The sheer size of this image, combined with a fluorescent pink background, gives this cover a tongue-in-cheek feel.

• Buy an inexpensive camera and experiment with taking your own photographs. Other than "found" photos, this can be the most cost-effective way to obtain photographic images.

• Find a photographer willing to exchange a reduced rate for a shoot for a prominent photo credit and samples of the finished piece. This can give you good photographs to work with and the photographer a portfolio piece to show to other clients.

Chapter Four
Low-Cost Production and Printing

One of the best ways to save money is to educate yourself about the ins and outs of the technical side of design—meaning production, printing and binding. You may have no interest in this side of design but, like knowing how to manage your money or fix your car, it behooves you to learn as much as you can.

Taking classes to get a technical foundation is, of course, just a start. Since the technology behind production, printing and binding continues to change rapidly from year to year, even designers who thought they were well-versed in these subjects are occasionally caught by surprise.

To keep up with these changes, design and computer books and magazines are a necessity. You might not have time to read every word, but even skimming through and reading just a portion will let you know what's going on in the industry.

Finally, talk to the pros; find a service bureau and a printer whose expertise you trust, and go to them with specific questions, even in the course of designing a job.

Learn how to cut costs on every phase of a piece.

Low-Cost Production

Efficiently using found or computer-produced type, copyright-free visuals and standard paper sizes are all effective ways to keep costs down. But there are several other things you can do to eliminate unnecessary steps in production to save time and money.

For instance, try to get your client to supply you with copy for the piece on disk, to avoid rekeying all of the copy on your computer. If your client's computer is compatible with yours, all the better; if not, invest in a file exchange program, or go to an instant printer who can convert the files to work with your computer. If both you and your client have a modem, this can be done even more quickly. If you don't have access to a computer and still have to use a typesetter, having your copy on disk will save time and money at that stage too.

If you are using a page layout program, there are a variety of time-saving templates (standardized layouts or grids) already set up for you in formats that range from brochures to newsletters. If you still want to create your own grid or layout, feel free; most page layout programs allow you to do that and to save these grids so you can use them again. If, for example, a client has commissioned you to do a newsletter four times a year, you can set up a standard style for that publication that includes established column widths, type styles, and the size and intensity of headings, subheadings and body copy. That way, when you go to work on the second and third editions, the design work and formatting have already been done. And anything that saves time saves money.

Two words of caution here: First,

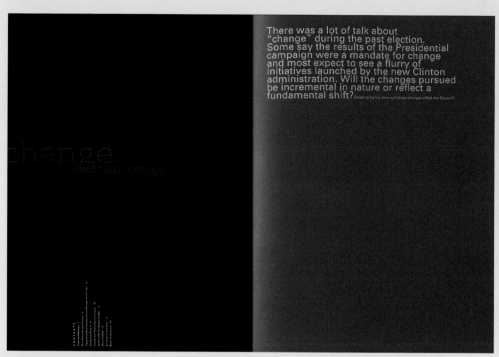

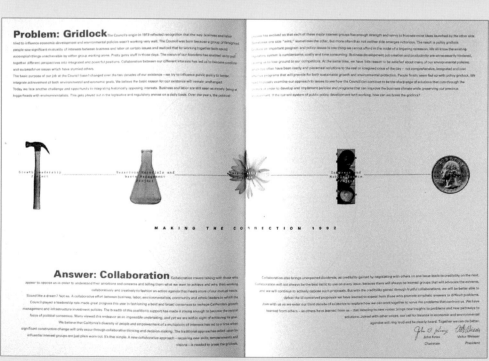

This annual report for the California Council had a minimal budget for photography, so existing photographs of objects were incorporated. To cut down on costs, typography—in combination with a dramatic black, white and red color scheme—was used to make a strong graphic impact.

Creating Great Designs on a Limited Budget

Using a logo and minimal typography, a suite of one-color collateral pieces was designed to promote the capabilities of Radio Gabby. To make an inexpensive but impressive presentation, a stock corrugated box was printed in one color and the various pieces were packed in waste paper from a document shredder.

remember to save intermediate versions of everything you're designing; some of your original ideas may prove to be your best. Second, don't fall prey to the trap of using the same format for too many different clients. While you may be able to look for similarities between new and previous projects, your work should be fresh and unique each time. Remember, the computer is only a tool, not a replacement for an original and creative idea.

Ways to cut production costs:

• Reduce the number of images you use within a piece; this not only cuts costs but may increase the impact of the visuals that remain.

• If you aren't working on a computer, use veloxes instead of halftones.

• Use a computer-generated illustration done on an illustration program. No intermediate reproduction—such as stats or scanning—will be needed, and the image can go straight to film.

• A design that uses type and graphics straight from the laser printer should be printed on a heavily textured stock to hide the roughness of the reproduction.

• Design with printing in mind; if a piece will be quick-printed, keep it simple to reduce the impact of less-than-perfect reproduction.

• Have your client carefully proofread copy before you typeset to save on corrections and alterations after the copy has been set.

• Establish simple computer templates for ongoing projects, and reuse them whenever appropriate.

Low-Cost Production

A flying book and a butterfly net makes a visual pun about "collecting."
The image was done on an illustration program and pulled directly into a
page layout program, avoiding the need for any intermediate reproduction
of the image. The poster is printed in two colors on colored paper, giving it
the look of a three-color job.

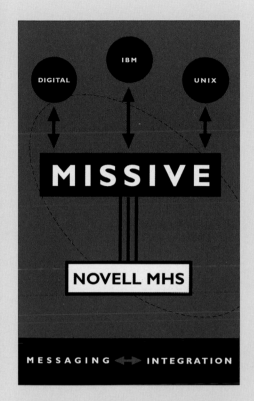

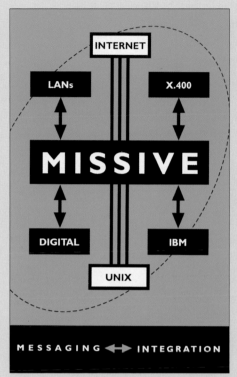

This group of related flow-chart-style posters was produced using nothing more than simple graphic elements found in a page layout program. A basic design was established, then subsequent versions of the poster were created by making minor alterations and additions. The addition of a different, bright second-color ensures that each piece will be distinct from the others.

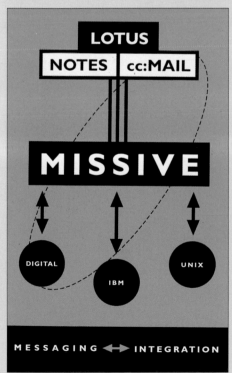

Adding Low-Cost Color

When you're limiting the number of colors used in your design to save money, you must select and use them carefully and appropriately. Both the ink and paper color you choose will help set the tone of the finished piece.

If you want to create a dramatic look, just use black and white. This bold approach may help you achieve the effect you're looking for. Another way to achieve a bold look is to use complementary colors—that is, colors that are opposite one another on the color wheel. Examples of this would be red and green or yellow and blue. Primary colors are simple and striking and tend to create a more exciting feeling than muted tones; they can be used for pieces associated with children, or even for institutional or industrial clients. Using warm and cool colors together can create an interesting effect.

Screens can expand the design capabilities of a one-color piece. Screened boxes behind important copy or photographs add visual interest and the suggestion of an additional color. Take care, however, not to use too many screens at too many different percentages; this may cheapen rather than enhance the look of the finished piece.

It's also possible to get increased mileage out of color by printing one or two different colors on each part of your piece—for instance, by printing a different color on each component of a letterhead system. Since the pieces are used together, this gives the impression of multi-colored printing, but is much less expensive than using all three colors on each piece. Another application of this can be used in producing a multi-page

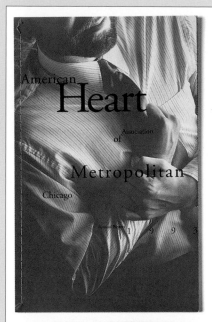

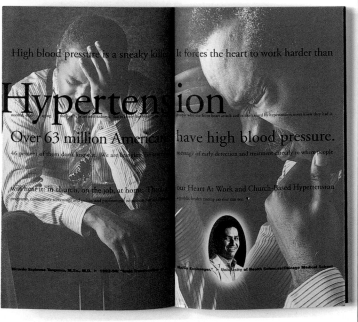

Duotoned photographs lend this annual report a richness of color and variety. Although printed in five colors, the designers saved money by printing the entire piece on one side of a single press sheet. The page spreads were folded blank side in, collated, and stitched on the front to give the piece an unusual binding. Since each single page is a double thickness of paper, the designers were able to use a less expensive grade of paper without sacrificing a quality "feel."

The designer has devised a system of colorful stickers that, when applied to a one-color piece, gives the appearance of many colors. Two sizes of the sticker were printed, one for stationery and business envelopes, and one for the business card and for large envelopes and mailers. The sticker can also be used as needed to brighten up the designer's self-promotional pieces, such as the moving announcement shown here.

booklet. Print one or two different colors on two different large sheets, then have them cut and bound with the pages of the two sheets merged to create a piece with many colors.

Another way to save on the cost of color is to use premixed or stock inks whenever possible. Most small printers have a variety of standard colors that cost less than special order colors. Some printers even have a scheduled arrangement to print specific colors on certain days of the week. If you can use these standard colors and have your job printed on the appropriate day, this can save you not only money, but possibly time, too. Maintaining files with cost lists and samples from a number of area printers will allow you maximum flexibility—and maximum cost savings—on all your print jobs. Be sure, though, that the color you choose will work effectively for your design.

You can also use your laser printer to produce pieces with color if your print run is small. You can produce an entire piece in, say, blue or red, just by putting a colored toner cartridge in your laser printer. Or, by using more than one colored cartridge, you can produce a two- or even three-color piece: Simply set up a layout for each color in a separate file, then run your paper through the printer two or three times, depending on how many colors you want to use. If you're using more than one color, pay close attention to proper registration, that is, where and how the colors meet or work next to each other. This will make the difference between a piece that looks professional and one that doesn't.

Split fountain printing can also enhance your piece without adding

Adding Low-Cost Color

considerably to your printing cost. Split fountain printing allows the printer to print two or more colors of ink from a single fountain on the press, creating an interesting graded effect that generally costs little more than a one-color job. If you're considering this, make sure to see samples of your printer's split fountain work, since, as with any other production technique, the quality with which this is done will affect the overall effectiveness of your finished piece.

Ink is only one way to add color to your designs. Using colored paper also allows you to add color to your piece. You have the option of printing the entire piece on one color of paper or, if the piece is multi-paged, to print only some flats on a color and the rest on another color, or on white. Be careful, however, to make sure that the ink colors you select will print well on the stock colors you choose. Since most inks are translucent, they print differently on colored paper than on white paper, so consult with your printer, and get a sample if possible.

For more information on getting the most from a limited color palette, see Mike Zender's *Getting Unlimited Impact with Limited Color.*

Techniques for stretching color dollars:

• When designing a two-color job, avoid using black. Just make sure one of the two colors is dark enough to make the smallest type legible; examples would be dark blue, olive green, burgundy or gray.

• Use spot color instead of traps or tight registration; the job will be easier to print, and therefore cheaper.

The idea of change is dramatically expressed here in a five-color split fountain. As the clients' corporate name changes from left to right, so does the color of the chameleon. Printed on one side and accordion folded, this piece cost only slightly more to print than a two-color job.

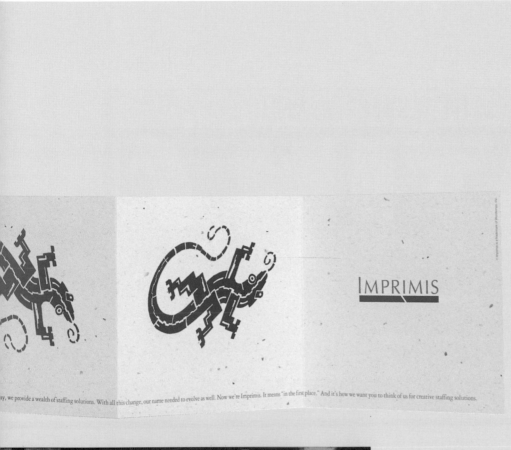

- Print one color of ink on a colored paper.

- If your print run is small, use rubber stamps, watercolors, colored pencils, markers or crayons to add color to your piece. Or design a piece specifically to be hand-colored.

- Vary colors of paper within a multi-page piece or series of pieces to add variety at no extra cost.

- Attach colored stickers to your piece—either ones you've found or ones you've produced yourself.

- Choose a brightly colored paper, such as one of the Astrobrights or Cross Pointe Brights.

- Use screen combinations of black and a match color.

- Overprint screens of two solid colors to make a third color.

- Print with a split fountain for little more than the cost of a single color.

- For very short-run color print jobs, use color photocopies.

- Tip in portions of four-color process pages or color photocopies as needed in a one- or two-color piece.

- Use premixed or stock inks when possible; this limits your color choices but saves you money.

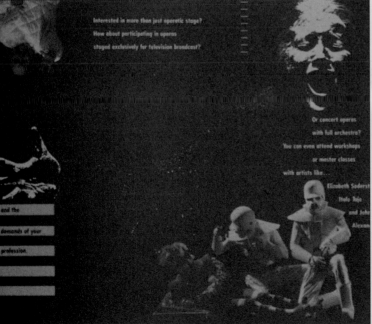

The combination of colored paper stock and two-color printing gives the effect of a piece with many colors. The ink colors change their appearance when combined with the different paper colors. There was no budget for photography, so the designer used existing publicity photos that the client had on file.

Adding Low-Cost Color

A successful use of split fountain printing gives the effect of several colors for little more than the cost of one. The ink trough was split and yellow and red inks were used, creating a blend of orange in the center. Black was overprinted to give the colors a luminous look.

Simple, computer-generated line art and split-fountain printing using two metallic colors produce an effect that belies the economy of this piece. Although this poster appears to have been printed in several colors, it cost just slightly more than printing one color. The printer's matte coated house stock was used to enhance the metallic effect.

Saving Money on Paper

If you're trying to keep costs down, one of the most important things you can do is to involve your printer in the design process. Information and expertise provided by your printer may help you avoid unnecessary costs, and even to cut some corners without sacrificing quality.

First, make sure to consult your printer about the size sheet the paper you are selecting comes in. Make sure the size of your piece fits within the parameters of a press sheet of stock to avoid paying for paper that will just be trimmed off your piece. Depending on the sheet size, you might consider reducing the size of your design to increase the number of pieces you can get from a parent sheet; sometimes making a design only one inch shorter will allow you to print two pieces from a single sheet instead of one. And in most cases, making a change like this will not adversely affect your piece.

If you must trim off something from a print job, utilize what's being trimmed off; for instance, if five inches will be trimmed off the side of a poster, print something else on the part that's trimmed off. A bookmark and a one-sided card-style invitation are two suggestions, but be creative. That extra paper may even allow you to create a self-promotion piece that you may not have been able to afford otherwise.

Avoid bleeds so your piece will fit on a stock sized sheet. If you are planning bleeds, authorize the printer to trim your piece to slightly under the usual or intended size. No one will notice that a finished piece is 8⅜ x 10⅞ inches instead of 8½ x 11 inches.

Another way to save money on

Pages in this piece are either one or two colors and were left unbound to facilitate easy updating without reprinting the entire piece. The pages that often need to be updated were printed as one-color blanks that can be laser-printed, then tucked into the two-color folder. The piece is bound together with a piece of corrugated cardboard and a thick red rubber band.

and Printing

Four two-color cards were economically ganged together on a single press sheet, collated and inserted into a two-color newsprint "envelope." The envelope was created by folding a square sheet of newsprint, avoiding the need for a die-cut.

paper is to use what's readily available rather than what has to be ordered. Printers often have leftover sheets from other jobs that you can get cheaply; if your printer has enough to spare, you may be able to get samples. You may find something affordable that precisely meets your needs, or something that suggests new and exciting design possibilities. Paper suppliers or wholesalers may also be a good source of leftover stock that can be purchased at a reasonable cost. Or, if your run is short, a stationery store can also be a good source of inexpensive, make ready paper.

Finally, consider unusual stocks and sources of paper; be creative. Print your pieces on construction paper, paper bags, or other unusual—and inexpensive—stock normally not used for design jobs. Also consider creative recycling of paper you already have—for instance, print your own self-promotional material on color proofs from old jobs. Or, if you've got the time and the inclination, learn to recycle overruns or paper trimmed off other printed pieces into handmade paper that you can use for invitations or self-promotional pieces.

You can also save money on printing. While the standard approach to many design projects involves offset printing, there are a number of ways to accomplish the desired results. For instance, when the number of completed pieces you need is relatively small, use a photocopier to produce them and hand-color or otherwise manipulate them after your copies are made. Silkscreen printing can also create an interesting effect where appropriate to your design,

Saving Money on Paper and Printing

giving colors a highly saturated, yet velvety, look; for small print runs, letterpress also gives a unique effect that's close to a very subtle embossment, but much cheaper.

Whatever printing method you use remember to proofread your copy carefully before submitting it for printing and at the proofing (blueline) stage. The farther into the production process you are, the more costly changes or corrections will be. This is especially true if you're working with an offset printer because of the costs associated with setting up and breaking down the press. If you're not a great proofreader, or if you've worked on a project so long you think you won't be able to see mistakes, find someone else to take a look at your piece. Even if you have to pay someone to do so, you'll end up saving money in the long run if you prevent a few costly mistakes.

Ways to cut printing costs:

• Have large scale, short-run projects screen printed.

• Print small-run pieces on letterpress.

• Use direct image-to-plate printing plates instead of negative and metal plates.

• Shop for paper at a stationery store or mill-end warehouse.

• Try to use standard sized press sheets; if you want to have a bleed, authorize the printer to trim your piece slightly under the usual size.

• On a small print run, switch to a cover weight stock to add "quality" to a piece.

• Choose a paper that comes with a

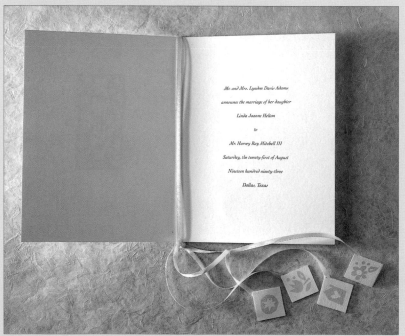

When a piece is produced in a limited quantity, you can consider a design that requires labor-intensive handwork. This wedding announcement, although an extremely simple one-color printing job, required four small square cards to be hand attached to the ends of two lengths of satin ribbon.

special effect, such as speckles, embossing, ridges, or a parchment that looks like clouds.

- Reduce the size of a piece to increase the number of pieces you can get from a parent sheet.

- Try to get dark color with ink, not paper; a dark stock will often cost more than a light one, and the printer may have to use an opaque ink beneath an area of color to cover the paper adequately, increasing the press time and amount of ink needed.

- Proof final artwork carefully; making changes after the printing process has begun raises costs dramatically.

- Use your printer's house stock. Your job can be printed less expensively since they buy their house stock in great quantity.

- Use leftover stock that the printer has on hand.

- Reduce the number of pages in a booklet or newsletter.

- Use mock "die-cuts" and hole drilling. Straight angles can be cut on a paper cutter without adding the cost of a die, but can look like a die-cut job. Hole punch drills come in different diameters, and can be used as inexpensive round die-cuts.

The client needed approximately twenty thousand mailers for a performance and one thousand brochures for general information about the company. Seven thousand sheets were printed with two colors on one side and one color on the other, with only one plate change on the one-color side. By combining this into one printing, the poster was a bonus and provided visual interest to the mailers and brochure.

Saving Money on Paper and Printing

The designer had a very limited budget for printing, but wanted to create a piece that was three-dimensional to convey the breadth of services offered by the client. This piece was printed in two colors on the printer's house cover stock, with the bulk of the budget used for a die-cut to create the two pop-out windows, the accordion fold, and the two straight cuts (to create the "roof tops") that were made after the piece was folded.

This surface of an actual striped bass was used to create the image used on this large scale poster. Ink was rolled onto the fish, and a direct transfer print was then made. The headline was drawn with a wet brush and text type was created on a computer. Silkscreened on wrinkled newsprint, the technique and materials reinforce a message about the imminent decay of San Francisco Bay.

Low Cost Binding

The process of binding a printed piece can add considerably to production costs. Some printers contract out for this work. Not only does this add time to the production process, but the printer will probably mark up the price and pass that cost on to you and your client. Finding alternative ways to bind your piece can save you both money and time.

If the quantity of pieces you're producing is small, you may want to bind them by hand. Pieces that are bound with ribbon, twine or string take on a unique, hand-produced appearance that may be especially appropriate to the tone you're trying to set. Consider this method and the materials you select carefully to make sure they're helping you accomplish your communication goals.

If you decide to have the piece bound professionally, consider one of the less costly methods. A saddle stitch, which is simply a stapled bind, is cheaper than a perfect bind, which finishes a booklet with an edge that is flat or at a right angle with the front and back cover. However, if your piece has too many pages, a saddle-stitched bind may not work for you; consult your printer. If you're printing on newsprint or a lightweight stock, and your piece doesn't have too many pages, you can even use a method that affixes small spots of glue rather than staples to hold the piece together. Again, this may not be appropriate in all cases, so consult your printer before selecting this method.

A GBC or spiral bind might also be appropriate for your piece. Both are less costly than a perfect bind; an additional advantage is that, since the pages are cut down to individual

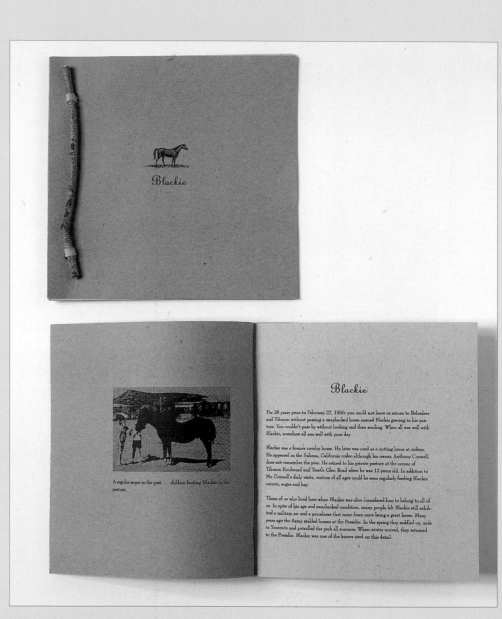

The designer was called upon to produce a low-budget, small quantity booklet for a benefit program. This piece was photocopied on kraft paper, and bound together with an elastic band and a twig—a binding that suits the rustic feel of the rest of the piece.

This piece was kept to two colors so the designer could splurge on a large format with spiral binding; this binding made it possible to include the vellum inserts printed in four-color as needed throughout the booklet.

sheets rather than attached to each other at the spine of the piece, these methods allow you to mix colors of paper at will. GBC and spirals also come in a variety of colors that can add interest to your piece. And because both GBC and spiral binds allow the piece (usually a book or booklet) to lay flat when open, they work well for books that need to stay open on their own, such as manuals or cookbooks. If you produce a lot of pieces that need to be spiral bound, consider investing in a spiral binder, which will enable you to spiral bind your own pieces whenever you want.

Ways to cut binding costs:

•   Tie folded page spreads together with twine, string or ribbon. A piece of rough, natural twine is ideal for an environmental piece, while a piece of silk ribbon would be appropriate for an elegant party invitation.

•   Hold multiple pages together with thick or thin colored rubber bands.

•   Put printed pieces in inexpensive boxes that you find or make yourself for a memorable presentation that reinforces the message inside.

•   Sew together pages of a thin booklet on a sewing machine.

•   Consider a multi-fold piece rather than separate pages that need to be trimmed, collated and saddle-stitched. This not only saves money but is more environmentally sound since it eliminates staples.

•   Alternative binding techniques—clamps, colored staples, rivets and paper clips—are effective ways to hold pages together, as long as they are appropriate to your design.

Striking a Deal

One of the best ways to cut the cost of producing a quality printed piece is to trade your own services for the materials and services you need to accomplish your goals. For example, many small printers offer design services to their customers, but few can afford on-staff, in-house designers. They often have to hire freelance designers to complete simple, routine jobs on a fairly regular basis. If you can fit this work into your schedule, your services could be exchanged for printing services, or at least a portion of them. This might also work with silkscreening, color separating, typesetting or any other business you need to get your work produced.

Deals also can be reached with other types of individuals and businesses. For instance, if you need a photograph but haven't budgeted for one, consider asking a photographer to trade the use of an existing photograph (with full credit to him on the piece) in exchange for a letterhead and business card design. This kind of arrangement can also work with illustrators, calligraphers, copywriters, or any other creative people who can help make your piece special. Seeking and maintaining collaborations with other creative people can have other benefits, too. You can recommend a photographer or illustrator friend to other designers, or they can recommend you to their clients.

If you're a freelance designer, there are even ways to strike up a deal with other designers, for instance, collaborating with other designers on a single piece near deadline time or sharing equipment or office space to keep your overhead down. This can be an ideal way to make expensive equipment such as

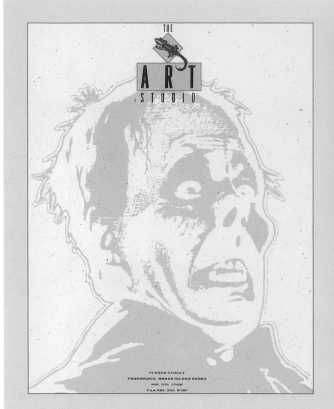

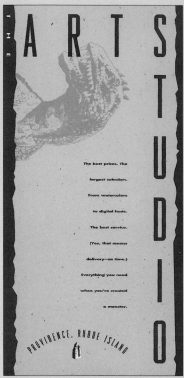

A small art supply store was in need of a new identity program, so it teamed up with a design studio to create these low-cost, high-quality promotional pieces. Production costs were kept to a minimum by using computer clip art and outputting directly to film. The pieces are printed in three colors, but appear to be more. The studio got art supplies that they needed in lieu of their design fee.

Creating Great Designs on a Limited Budget

A great example of group effort, the members of this studio got together to produce this holiday cookie package to give to clients and friends. The design of the packaging, all handwork, and even baking the cookies was a team endeavor. Consider projects like this a way to strike a deal with your own staff.

scanners more affordable.

Many arrangements like this can be made with some creative thinking and the willingness to broach the subject with another party. Usually, it's easy to determine what you want or need from another party, but more difficult to determine what you have that they might want. If you can't figure this out, ask them. It may save you some money and allow you to create a finished piece that's great rather than adequate.

Ways to "barter" to get pieces produced inexpensively:

• Offer a fledgling photographer or illustrator prominent credit on a piece in exchange for one-time use of their work.

• Offer your design services to a typesetting service or a desktop publishing bureau in exchange for their goods or services.

• If a piece is designed to showcase a printer's capabilities, work out a deal where the printer will print it for free in exchange for using it as a publicity piece.

• If a printer feels that the piece you've designed is for a good cause, they may offer a reduced price in exchange for a credit on the piece.

• Offer your design services at a reduced rate or on a pro bono basis to a client you deem worthy. They pay for printing, and you get a portfolio piece.

• Strike a deal with your own client to have them provide hand coloring, assembly or hand binding of their pieces to keep costs down.

Striking a Deal

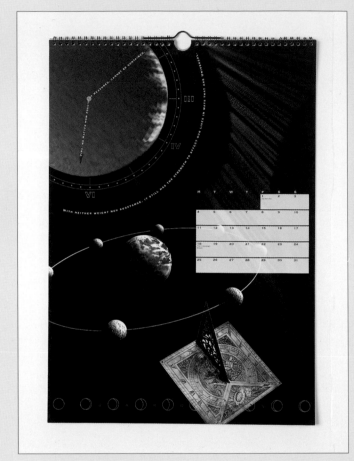

Collaborations between designers and printers are often very lavish and unusual, as both parties get to show off their capabilities with few budget constraints. This calendar was created as a promotional piece for the printer, but the design studio struck a deal to reduce their fee in exchange for enough calendars to send to their own clients.

The studio needed a small quantity of Christmas cards to send to clients. They traded their services with a printer who could do letterpress, a process that lends a unique old-fashioned look to a piece, but would have been extremely expensive in large quantities. The torn edge and binding was done by hand by studio staff.

Chapter Five
More Great Designs on a Limited Budget

Now that you've seen the principles and techniques employed in designing good pieces on a limited budget, let's look at more work by design studios that didn't let a lack of funds curtail their creativity.

You'll see many of the tips that were set forth in previous chapters put into action in this chapter—sometimes singly, sometimes with a number of techniques utilized within a single piece. These uses will be quite evident sometimes, but more often will be invisible. You won't notice techniques such as well-planned production or effective use of existing photographs, because their uses will be integrated so seamlessly into the piece itself.

Don't compare the effectiveness of your low-budget projects to projects such as the big-budget paper promotions you see in the annuals; instead compare them to pieces like the ones in this chapter (and for that matter, throughout this book), where designers worked under the same constraints you're working under, and still came up winners. Use these examples for tips you can incorporate into your own work, but also use them for inspiration that—for designers with the right ideas and the right skills to execute them well—great design is possible no matter how low your budget.

See how other designers have made the most of their limited budgets.

More Great Designs

Although this self-promotional piece is silkscreened in five colors on a good quality T-shirt, the artist saved money by keeping the artwork simple and easy to produce. The shirt is packaged in an attractive and economical stock corrugated box with a sticker bearing the designer's logo applied to the front. Considering the attention garnered when the recipient wore the shirt, this piece is a good example of getting a lot of impact for a little money.

ROBERT RAUSCHENBERG

**THE ALGUR
H. MEADOWS
AWARD FOR
EXCELLENCE IN
THE ARTS**

**The Meadows School of the Arts
at Southern Methodist University in Dallas** established the
Algur H. Meadows Award
For Excellence in the Arts
in 1978 to recognize the
highest level of interna-
tional achievement in the
creative and performing
arts. The Award honors the
accomplishments of an
artist and provides a fo-
rum to share ideas and
aspirations with the Dallas
community.

Previous recipients of
the Algur H. Meadows
Award For Excellence in
the Arts include: Ingmar
Bergman, Martha Gra-
ham, John Houseman,
Mstislav Rostropovich, and
Merce Cunningham. The
sixth recipient, Robert
Rauschenberg, will be in-
residence on the SMU cam-
pus November 4-8, when
he will be presented with
the Award.

You are cordially invited
to join us for a series of
lectures entitled "Images:
Between Art and Life" with
curators, critics, photo-
graphers, musicians, printers, artists, filmmakers and
poets; and for the exhibition, "A Tribute to Rauschenberg."

All events are free and
open to the public. For
additional information,
call 214/692-ARTS.

▶

For a newsletter featuring an article
on the artist Robert Rauschenberg, a
small photograph of him was blown
up to gigantic proportions on a photocopy machine. The process produced
a gritty, textural effect and allowed
the image to be reproduced as line art
rather than a halftone.

More Great Designs

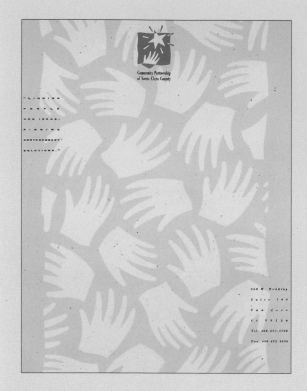

Using the hand in the logo as a simple overall pattern, a texture is created by reversing this image out of a screen of color, so that the image takes on the color of the stock. Each component of the stationery system is only two colors, but because the second color on each piece is different, the overall look is of many colors. Since each piece is printed separately, changing the second color on each adds very little to the cost.

The past six years have been an exciting time of growth and discovery for the Getty Center for Education in the Arts. This is our first newsletter, and with it we hope to bring you up to date on some of the things that have happened and on the progress of the Center's programs.

It's no secret that we are in the midst of a national movement to reform education in this country and that a part of this movement is a growing support for expanding the role of art education in the schools. Educators, public officials, and parents have come to share the view that the arts can and must have a more significant place in the education of children.

"A painter takes the sun and makes it into a yellow spot.

An artist takes a yellow spot and makes it into a sun."

PABLO PICASSO

The study of the visual arts has generally occupied a marginal niche in the school curriculum. The public frequently regards art education as a recreational activity, and school authorities often find it convenient to abandon art programs in cost-cutting periods. Consequently, most American students graduate from high school having had only the most cursory exposure to art.

We believe that the Center can contribute to improving the status and quality of art education in the schools. At the outset, it adopted an approach called discipline-based art education (DBAE for short) which broadens art education by integrating ideas and skills from four disciplines: art history, art criticism, and aesthetics in a sequential written curriculum.

We are pleased to have played an active part in helping to form new partnerships and advocacy groups on behalf of DBAE. We are especially encouraged to find enthusiastic support for these efforts from so many different groups representing such diverse constituencies.

With a new and complex approach to education, there are bound to be misunderstandings about DBAE. We hope that this newsletter, in addition to being a progress report, will help clarify many of the issues involved in DBAE as well as provide fresh information for those who seek to become more familiar with it.

Leilani Lattin Duke
The Getty Center for Education in the Arts

Combining "found" line cuts and original art is often a good solution when producing a monthly newsletter. The top left and center sunbursts are antique line cuts, while the others were created by the designers. Using this technique, you can create a custom look while saving time and money.

More Great Designs

When skillfully used, three colors of ink can yield very dramatic results. Blue, yellow and magenta combine here to produce a wide variety of colors. Halftones have been layered over each other to give an incredible feeling of depth.

Copyright-free black-and-white ad cuts from the 1940s are used here to convey the theme of a competition, "Creating Magic through Public Relations." Creative use of the ad cuts, enlarging, reducing, overlapping and adding color produces a feeling of excitement.

More Great Designs

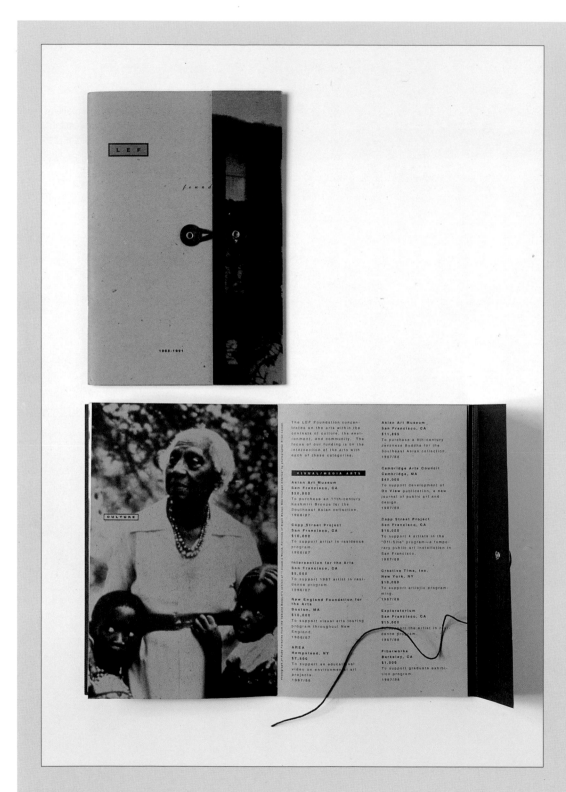

A unique grommet and string closure accents this otherwise inexpensive piece. The designer made a conscious decision to spend part of the budget on the attention-getting closure rather than adding another color or using more expensive paper.

SEATTLE CAMERATA

WORLD-CLASS ARTISTS IN INTIMATE SETTINGS

Ridge String Quartet
Dome Room, The Arctic Building
November 9, 1991

Magical Strings
Franklin High School
March 7, 1992

Scholars of London
Grand Central Arcade
January 26, 1992

Golub-Kaplan-Carr Trio
Seattle Art Museum
March 29, 1992

Seattle Chamber Players
Chinese Room, Smith Tower
February 9, 1992

Duane Hulbert, Pianist
Columbia Winery, Woodinville
May 1, 1992

The designer was faced with the problem of making a piece look opulent to match its message, but doing it on a budget. A three-color split-fountain printing job produced an expensive-looking piece that cost slightly more than a one-color job. The swirl pattern in the background was created by screening.

Index

Creating Great Designs on a Limited Budget